Approaches to learning and teaching

History

a toolkit for international teachers

Andrew Flint and Stuart Jack

Series Editors: Paul Ellis and Lauren Harris

CAMBRIDGE
UNIVERSITY PRESS

University Printing House, Cambridge CB2 8BS, United Kingdom

One Liberty Plaza, 20th Floor, New York, NY 10006, USA

477 Williamstown Road, Port Melbourne, VIC 3207, Australia

314–321, 3rd Floor, Plot 3, Splendor Forum, Jasola District Centre, New Delhi – 110025, India

79 Anson Road, #06–04/06, Singapore 079906

Cambridge University Press is part of the University of Cambridge.

It furthers the University's mission by disseminating knowledge in the pursuit of education, learning and research at the highest international levels of excellence.

www.cambridge.org
Information on this title: www.cambridge.org/9781108439879 (Paperback)

© Cambridge Assessment International Education 2018

® IGCSE is a registered trademark

First published 2018

20 19 18 17 16 15 14 13 12 11 10 9 8 7 6 5 4 3 2 1

Printed in Great Britain by CPI Group (UK) Ltd, Croydon CR0 4YY

A catalogue record for this publication is available from the British Library

ISBN 978-1-108-43987-9 Paperback

Contents

Online lesson ideas for this book can be found at cambridge.org/9781108439879

Acknowledgements

The authors and publishers acknowledge the following sources of copyright material and are grateful for the permissions granted. While every effort has been made, it has not always been possible to identify the sources of all the material used, or to trace all copyright holders. If any omissions are brought to our notice, we will be happy to include the appropriate acknowledgements on reprinting.

Thanks to the following for permission to reproduce images:

Fig. 3.2 Galerie Bilderwelt/Hulton Archive/Getty Images; Fig. 4.1 Klaus Lang/All Canada Photos/Getty Images; Fig. 4.2 Everett Collection, Inc./ Alamy Stock Photo; Fig. 7.2 Mint Images – David Arky/Getty Images; Fig. 7.3 View Stock/Getty Images; Fig. 8.2 Apic/RETIRED/Hulton Archive/Getty Images; Fig. 12.1 Print Collector/Hulton Archive/Getty Images; Fig. 12.2 Print Collector/Hulton Archive/Getty Images.

Introduction to the series by the editors

1

1 Approaches to learning and teaching History

This series of books is the result of close collaboration between Cambridge University Press and Cambridge Assessment International Education, both departments of the University of Cambridge. The books are intended as a companion guide for teachers, to supplement your learning and provide you with extra resources for the lessons you are planning. Their focus is deliberately not syllabus-specific, although occasional reference has been made to programmes and qualifications. We want to invite you to set aside for a while assessment objectives and grading, and take the opportunity instead to look in more depth at how you teach your subject and how you motivate and engage with your students.

The themes presented in these books are informed by evidence-based research into what works to improve students' learning and pedagogical best practices. To ensure that these books are first and foremost practical resources, we have chosen not to include too many academic references, but we have provided some suggestions for further reading.

We have further enhanced the books by asking the authors to create accompanying lesson ideas. These are described in the text and can be found in a dedicated space online. We hope the books will become a dynamic and valid representation of what is happening now in learning and teaching in the context in which you work.

Our organisations also offer a wide range of professional development opportunities for teachers. These range from syllabus- and topic-specific workshops and large-scale conferences to suites of accredited qualifications for teachers and school leaders. Our aim is to provide you with valuable support, to build communities and networks, and to help you both enrich your own teaching methodology and evaluate its impact on your students.

Each of the books in this series follows a similar structure. In the third chapter, we have asked our authors to consider the essential elements of their subject, the main concepts that might be covered in a school curriculum, and why these are important. The next chapters give you a brief guide on how to interpret a syllabus or subject guide, and how to plan a programme of study. The authors will encourage you to think too about what is not contained in a syllabus and how you can pass on your own passion for the subject you teach.

The main body of the text takes you through those aspects of learning and teaching which are widely recognised as important. We would like to stress that there is no single recipe for excellent teaching, and that different schools, operating in different countries and cultures, will have strong traditions that should be respected. There is a growing consensus, however, about some important practices and approaches that need to be adopted if students are going to fulfil their potential and be prepared for modern life.

In the common introduction to each of these chapters, we look at what the research says and the benefits and challenges of particular approaches. Each author then focuses on how to translate theory into practice in the context of their subject, offering practical lesson ideas and teacher tips. These chapters are not mutually exclusive but can be read independently of each other and in whichever order suits you best. They form a coherent whole but are presented in such a way that you can dip into the book when and where it is most convenient for you to do so.

The final two chapters are common to all the books in this series and are not written by the subject authors. After the subject context chapters, we include guidance on how to reflect on your teaching and some avenues you might explore to develop your own professional learning. Schools and educational organisations are increasingly interested in the impact that classroom practice has on student outcomes. We have therefore included an exploration of this topic and some practical advice on how to evaluate the success of the learning opportunities you are providing for your students.

We hope you find these books accessible and useful. We have tried to make them conversational in tone so you feel we are sharing good practice rather than directing it. Above all, we hope that the books will inspire you and enable you to think in more depth about how you teach and how your students learn.

Paul Ellis and Lauren Harris

Series Editors

2 | Purpose and context

International research into educational effectiveness tells us that student achievement is influenced most by what teachers do in classrooms. In a world of rankings and league tables we tend to notice performance, not preparation, yet the product of education is more than just examinations and certification. Education is also about the formation of effective learning habits that are crucial for success within and beyond the taught curriculum.

The purpose of this series of books is to inspire you as a teacher to reflect on your practice, try new approaches and better understand how to help your students learn. We aim to help you develop your teaching so that your students are prepared for the next level of their education as well as life in the modern world.

This book will encourage you to examine the processes of learning and teaching, not just the outcomes. We will explore a variety of teaching strategies to enable you to select which is most appropriate for your students and the context in which you teach. When you are making your choice, involve your students: all the ideas presented in this book will work best if you engage your students, listen to what they have to say, and consistently evaluate their needs.

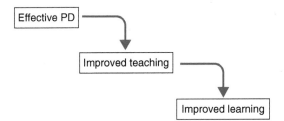

Cognitive psychologists, coaches and sports writers have noted how the aggregation of small changes can lead to success at the highest level. As teachers, we can help our students make marginal gains by guiding them in their learning, encouraging them to think and talk about how they are learning, and giving them the tools to monitor their success. If you take care of the learning, the performance will take care of itself.

When approaching an activity for the first time, or revisiting an area of learning, ask yourself if your students know how to:

* approach a new task and plan which strategies they will use
* monitor their progress and adapt their approach if necessary
* look back and reflect on how well they did and what they might do differently next time.

2 Approaches to learning and teaching History

Effective students understand that learning is an active process. We need to challenge and stretch our students and enable them to interrogate, analyse and evaluate what they see and hear. Consider whether your students:

- challenge assumptions and ask questions
- try new ideas and take intellectual risks
- devise strategies to overcome any barriers to their learning that they encounter.

As we discuss in Chapter 6 **Active learning** and Chapter 8 **Metacognition**, it is our role as teachers to encourage these practices with our students so that they become established routines. We can help students review their own progress as well as getting a snapshot ourselves of how far they are progressing by using some of the methods we explore in Chapter 7 on **Assessment for Learning**.

Students often view the subject lessons they are attending as separate from each other, but they can gain a great deal if we encourage them to take a more holistic appreciation of what they are learning. This requires not only understanding how various concepts in a subject fit together, but also how to make connections between different areas of knowledge and how to transfer skills from one discipline to another. As our students successfully integrate disciplinary knowledge, they are better able to solve complex problems, generate new ideas and interpret the world around them.

In order for students to construct an understanding of the world and their significance in it, we need to lead students into thinking habitually about why a topic is important on a personal, local and global scale. Do they realise the implications of what they are learning and what they do with their knowledge and skills, not only for themselves but also for their neighbours and the wider world? To what extent can they recognise and express their own perspective as well as the perspectives of others? We will consider how to foster local and global awareness, as well as personal and social responsibility, in Chapter 12 on **Global thinking**.

As part of the learning process, some students will discover barriers to their learning: we need to recognise these and help students to overcome them. Even students who regularly meet success face their own challenges. We have all experienced barriers to our own learning at some point in our lives and should be able as teachers to empathise and share our own methods for dealing with these.

In Chapter 10 **Inclusive education** we discuss how to make learning accessible for everyone and how to ensure that all students receive the instruction and support they need to succeed as students.

Some students are learning through the medium of English when it is not their first language, while others may struggle to understand subject jargon even if they might otherwise appear fluent. For all students, whether they are learning through their first language or an additional language, language is a vehicle for learning. It is through language that students access the content of the lesson and communicate their ideas. So, as teachers, it is our responsibility to make sure that language isn't a barrier to learning. In Chapter 9 on **Language awareness** we look at how teachers can pay closer attention to language to ensure that all students can access the content of a lesson.

Alongside a greater understanding of what works in education and why, we (as teachers) can also seek to improve how we teach and expand the tools we have at our disposal. For this reason, we have included Chapter 11 **Teaching with digital technologies**, discussing what this means for our classrooms and for us as teachers. Institutes of higher education and employers want to work with students who are effective communicators and who are information literate. Technology brings both advantages and challenges and we invite you to reflect on how to use it appropriately.

This book has been written to help you think harder about the impact of your teaching on your students' learning. It is up to you to set an example for your students and to provide them with opportunities to celebrate success, learn from failure and, ultimately, to succeed.

We hope you will share what you gain from this book with other teachers and that you will be inspired by the ideas that are presented here. We hope that you will encourage your school leaders to foster a positive environment that allows both you and your students to meet with success and to learn from mistakes when success is not immediate. We hope too that this book can help in the creation and continuation of a culture where learning and teaching are valued and through which we can discover together what works best for each and every one of our students.

3 | The nature of the subject

Why is History important?

In History, we meet characters more extraordinary and varied than can even be found in Shakespeare's plays. There is romance, adventure, intrigue and beauty. There are issues as subtle and complex as any that can be conceived. We deal with town and country, home and abroad, local and national, spiritual and material.

The world is full of people who want us to believe what they say and to share their views and values. Politicians, journalists and advertisers are obvious examples. In order to have a deeper and wider perspective in the modern world, we must keep exercising our minds to enable us to test the pronouncements and the judgements of others. History trains us to be healthily sceptical so that we can ask important questions in the modern world.

The Oxford historian Theodore Zeldin once argued that 'history is autobiography'. In other words, as one learns about other people, one learns about oneself. Through our learning, we put ourselves within a wider perspective. We recognise that there have been intelligent, honest and good people in other ages, whose prejudices, attitudes and ideas are different from our own. As such, History teaches tolerance, flexibility, openness and awareness. To study History is to become a more complete human being.

Who teaches History?

Although most History teachers will have a strong foundation of study in this subject, many may find themselves teaching History from a wide range of different backgrounds. For example, some will have focused on different subject areas or have studied a more broadly based arts course.

This can prove rather intimidating if you are required to teach a topic or a period where you lack a rigorous framework. However, do remember that almost all History teachers will have been required to teach periods where they have felt more insecure in their subject knowledge. The key in such cases is to develop a clear overview of the main topics or questions and then to establish a broad foundation of understanding. Most History teachers will have benefited from the generosity of other colleagues in sharing their resources, and are therefore prepared to do the same to help others new to the profession or those teaching unfamiliar courses.

Why do we study History?

Many students will find their History lessons hugely rewarding and interesting, but may question the wider purpose of studying History. There are lots of justifications which may be explored for the study and teaching of the subject.

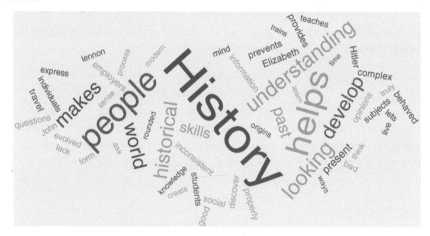

Figure 3.1: Diagram of study.

LESSON IDEA 3.1 WHY DOES HISTORY MATTER?

One approach is to investigate the importance and justification of historical study. You could also explore the consequences of the abuse or falsification of History.

As an example, in 2000, David Irving brought a court action for libel against a historian, Deborah Lipstadt, and her publisher, Penguin Books. Lipstadt had described Irving as a 'dangerous spokesperson' for Holocaust denial. In the resulting court case in London, Irving's legal action was rejected, with Judge Gray stating that Irving had 'for his own ideological reasons persistently and deliberately misrepresented and manipulated historical evidence'.

→

This can be a fascinating project study for why History matters. You can find more information online using the search term 'Irving v Lipstadt'.

Some useful arguments which were put forward by Arthur Marwick to justify the study of History are as follows:

1 History is interesting. This alone is enough to justify its study.
2 History helps us to develop a deeper understanding of peoples and cultures all around the world.
3 Everyone has a deep and powerful need to learn about and understand their past, both personally and collectively.
4 History provides valuable training for the mind. It helps us to present and assess arguments in a logical and systematic fashion, and therefore helps the development of skills vital for careers in areas such as law and journalism.
5 History helps us to understand and address the problems of modern societies.
6 Understanding the past can act as a guide to the future.

🖥 LESSON IDEA ONLINE 3.2: JUSTIFICATIONS FOR THE STUDY OF HISTORY
Use this lesson idea to stimulate discussion among your students about possible justifications for the study of History.

History and skills

History helps us to develop a wide range of critical skills which are transferable to many fields, such as:

- training in the selection and evaluation of evidence
- the capacity to examine and assess judgements
- the ability to synthesise a wide range of material into one coherent account
- the ability to present results clearly in prose and graphic form

- the ability to construct a logical argument and solve a problem with detailed evaluation
- the effective use of libraries, indexes, catalogues and internet resources.

Teacher Tip

Ask your students at the start of their courses what useful skills they believe they have to aid their historical studies, and which areas they think they will develop. You could extend this idea to look at some of the careers where these skills would be especially useful.

Interdisciplinary nature of History

Because of the range of issues examined in the History classroom, many teachers will seek to collaborate with their colleagues to explore joint themes and produce resources. As such, it can be extremely helpful for History teachers to have a clear understanding of the nature and progression of courses in other subjects.

The study of the First World War may be a particularly useful area for a more interdisciplinary, collaborative approach. For example, teachers can explore some of the following themes by working with teachers of other subjects in a First World War week:

- Literary works produced during, and inspired by, the war. (Literature)
- Works of art and music produced during or as a reaction to the war. (Art and Music)
- How the landscape shaped the nature of warfare. (Geography)
- How patterns of commemoration differed after the war. (Religious Studies/Global Perspectives)
- How gunners used mathematics to calibrate their artillery. (Mathematics)

The scope of the discipline

There are many aspects of historical exploration which can be integrated in a school or college History course. As such, it is often productive to have a range of different elements of the discipline incorporated into fields of study. Many courses in schools have a very strong emphasis on political and military history; nevertheless, it is important to provide students with a wider appreciation of the full scope of the discipline. For example, the spark which really captured the interest of one of my former students was the study of History and football. He produced a project on how football had been used for propaganda purposes in Spain, Italy and Germany and then went on to look at the career of the Brazilian footballer and political activist Socrates in the 1980s.

In short, look for opportunities to examine aspects of social, economic and gender history. We shall explore some of these areas through a series of lesson tips and ideas.

Gender

So much of the History studied in schools is very much *his*-story, with little focus on the experience of women. However, there are many ways to redress this balance, with the study of women in totalitarian regimes being particularly fruitful. Examining the lives of women in Germany, Russia or China during the twentieth century would enable you to assess how far women's opportunities and status were elevated or undermined in left- and right-wing states. A comparison of the treatment of women in a left- and a right-wing state would be a very productive approach.

LESSON IDEA 3.3 WOMEN AND THE NAZI STATE

Women have often been presented as the victims of the Nazis, but in recent years, more emphasis has been placed on women's roles as perpetrators of Nazism; in more sophisticated arguments, women have been viewed as often falling into both categories. You could challenge the view that women were simply the victims of Nazism using an image, such as the one in Figure 3.2.

→

Figure 3.2: Women overseers (Aufseherinnen) worked at the Belsen-Bergen concentration camp. This image follows their arrest by British troops in 1945.

Economic History

Some students will enjoy the opportunity to manipulate data to examine the relative success or failure of different economic policies. The study of the Soviet Union under communism provides plenty of scope to assess figures for the success of the New Economic Policy (NEP), the impact of the Five-Year Plans or even Khrushchev's economic de-Stalinisation or Gorbachev's Perestroika. Similarly, investigations of the Four-Year Plan in Germany or Mao's Five-Year Plans and policy of collectivisation may be effective. All these topics provide opportunities to evaluate the validity of economic data.

Art and History

The study of a period or a regime through its art may also be a successful exercise. If you are studying twentieth-century topics, consider looking at a range of works of art to illustrate the values of differing totalitarian regimes or reactions to them. Many teachers will have used paintings, such as Picasso's *Guernica* or *Weeping Woman*, for example, in teaching the Spanish Civil War. However, this is a good opportunity to work with colleagues in the Art department of your school to look at the work of some lesser-known artists.

☑ **LESSON IDEA ONLINE 3.4 USING ART IN THE CLASSROOM**

Use this lesson idea to encourage students to use sources from art to enrich their study of historical topics. The lesson examines Picasso's *Weeping Woman* (and optionally *Guernica*) in conjunction with the Spanish Civil War, but it could be adapted to fit other topics.

A final word

Dr Ben Dodds of Durham University in the UK wrote the following about the importance of the study of History. Think about giving his comments to your students to discuss, too.

> Historians have great responsibility in their exploration of knowledge: we must try to understand where the knowledge comes from, why we are exploring it and the uses to which it might be put. What is more, we must encourage others to treat historical knowledge in the same way.

Summary

In this chapter we have discussed the following:

- We hope all students enjoy the study of History, but they should also understand its importance. As History teachers, we have an obligation to work towards this aim.

- Students should be able to understand how the skills they develop in historical study will help them in many other ways.

- Developing an appreciation of the links and connections between different subject areas will deepen students' understanding of the past.

4 | Key considerations

Key considerations in teaching History

As History teachers, we all wish to inspire our students to develop a deep personal commitment to the subject, but we also seek to help them cultivate higher order skills of historical analysis and assessment. In this chapter, we shall explore some practical strategies to both focus your teaching and help students of all abilities develop interests and skills which will help them understand both the past and the present. As Simon Schama so aptly put it:

> Unless they can be won to History, their imagination will be held hostage in the cage of eternal **Now**: the flickering instant that's gone as soon as it has arrived. They will thus remain, as Cicero warned, 'permanent children, forever innocent of whence they have come and correspondingly unconcerned or, worse, fatalistic about where they might end up'.
>
> Simon Schama (*The Guardian*, 'My Vision for History in Schools', 9 November 2010)

Thinking about causation

Students' natural curiosity will lead them to question why events have unfolded in a particular way. What caused the First and Second World Wars? What were the causes of the revolutions in Russia in 1917? What caused and ended the Cold War?

So, how can we help to develop students' confidence in exploring issues of causation in an increasingly sophisticated manner? Here are some key issues to consider:

- How can you work with your students to develop approaches to causation which could help them appreciate how and why events took place?

- How can you help your students build hierarchies of different causal factors?
- How can students view different causal factors as part of a process of evaluating differing interpretations?

Examining causation is a good way to help students reflect with greater care on the language they use to describe and analyse differing causal relationships. This can be a key opportunity to help students develop a vocabulary bank to deepen their conceptual understanding. Often looking at the causes of very recent events can be a productive starting point to use a wider range of vocabulary to describe different types or levels of causation:

- What terms can students use to describe the relative importance of different causal factors?
- Is a factor fundamental or of lesser importance?
- Can students differentiate between long-term causes as opposed to trigger events?

Teacher Tip

Many students find it helpful to represent their ideas about causation visually, especially as flow diagrams. These can then be colour-coded to represent different types of causal factors.

LESSON IDEA 4.1: EXPLORING CAUSES OF CONFLICT

The first Gulf War is a useful topic to explore the nature of political and economic causes of conflict. Students could begin by looking at the long- and short-term political causes of the war before moving on to examine economic considerations; this could then lead to an assessment of the relative importance of different factors.

Thinking about change and continuity

Developing an appreciation of change and continuity is central in building students' historical understanding. However, these are some of the most challenging skills to work towards as they require the ability to cultivate a sense of overview. If students are to have a strong grasp of these issues, they must have a secure contextual framework with both breadth and depth of historical knowledge on which to build. Timelines and charts can be useful tools in establishing firm foundations.

Here are some goals for you to work towards with your students:

- Develop an appreciation of change and continuity with regard to political, social, economic and cultural developments.
- Develop an understanding of the nature and pace of historical change.
- Reflect on the nature and significance of turning points.
- Promote strategies to build your students' vocabulary with close examination of terms, such as 'evolution' and 'revolution'.

Teacher Tip

Some students may assume that change always means progress! Of course, this is not necessarily the case, so you need to emphasise the fluctuating nature of historical change. A good way to do this is to use charts and graphs to record changes over an extended period. This can enable students to make comparisons and form judgements about the positive or negative effects of change.

Thinking about significance

One of the most challenging tasks facing History teachers is helping their students to consider and assess the relative significance of processes, events and individuals. Questions of significance are often highly complex, so use this as an opportunity to develop higher order thinking and evaluative skills. If a student is to engage with questions of this nature, they will need to be able to think carefully about the strengths and limitations of different historical interpretations too. These are skills which can reflect a student's creativity and historical imagination. We shall be touching on some of these ideas further in Chapter 8 **Metacognition**.

▣ LESSON IDEA ONLINE 4.2: ASSESSING THE ROLES OF INDIVIDUALS

Many students find it challenging to assess the significance of events or individuals. Use this lesson to encourage students to consider what criteria can be used to assess significance.

LESSON IDEA 4.3: HISTORY AND PLACE NAMES

Another useful strategy is to examine place or street names in your nearest town and city (see Figure 4.1 for an example). Who are streets or squares named after, and why? Students might enjoy discussing similarities or differences in their criteria for assessing the significance of events or individuals.

An alternative approach might be to look at cities whose names have changed, such as modern day Ho Chi Minh City or St Petersburg.

Figure 4.1: Nelson Mandela Square, Sandton Johannesburg

Thinking about historical interpretations

Many students enjoy historical debate and recognise that there are often widely differing historical interpretations. An example might be: 'To what extent was Fidel Castro's rise to power a product of his own charismatic authority as opposed to the failings of Fulgencio Batista?'

How can we help our students evaluate the strengths and limitations of differing historical interpretations? Students must appreciate that historical interpretations are not absolute judgements but rather representations of the past, and are therefore open to scrutiny and debate. Our task as History teachers is to create a framework to ensure that our students' evaluation is rooted in historical evidence. We can do this by showing students that they should:

- be able to understand the central elements in a particular interpretation
- aim to use specific evidence to support and/or challenge historical interpretations
- seek to understand how a particular interpretation developed
- aim to assess the criteria on which to evaluate different historical interpretations.

Be careful to ensure your study of historical interpretations is based on a grasp of evidence. Many students can describe different historical interpretations and can attribute these to particular historians, such as 'Clark argued' or 'Evans stated'. Superficially this can seem impressive, but remember that we must maintain our focus on the strengths and weaknesses of the arguments rather than on a description of the debate itself.

LESSON IDEA 4.4: EXPLORING ECONOMIC HISTORY

Many courses examining Russian History will include some examination of the debate as to the success of Soviet economic policies in the 1930s.

→

Approaches to learning and teaching History

It is important to encourage your students to reflect on what 'success' means. They could examine a range of sources, both primary and secondary, which provide evidence for the impact of collectivisation and industrialisation. It is important to avoid crude judgements on these interpretations. Encourage students to develop their skills of synthesis in reaching an overall assessment on the question.

Teacher Tip

Film can be an excellent resource to examine different historical interpretations. A stimulating exercise would be to compare cinematic representations of Gandhi with other sources of historical evidence (Figure 4.2).

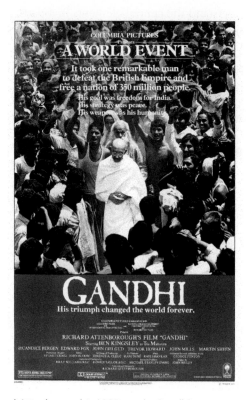

Figure 4.2: Richard Attenborough's 1982 movie *Gandhi*.

We will return to the skills required to evaluate historical interpretations in Chapter 5 **Interpreting a syllabus**, Chapter 8 **Metacognition** and Chapter 9 **Language awareness**.

Summary

In this chapter, we have examined the following strategies to develop your students' historical skills:

- balancing the teaching of historical content with the development of historical skills

- developing students' understanding of causation

- strengthening students' awareness of patterns of change and continuity

- helping students to improve their grasp of significance

- developing students' understanding and evaluation of historical interpretations.

5 | Interpreting a syllabus

What is a syllabus?

A syllabus is a document that sets out what you need to teach to students for a given course. For younger students, you and your school will usually plan what is going to be included on the syllabus. For students who are sitting external examinations, the syllabus will be provided by an examination board or education ministry; the syllabus documents are usually available online and it is best to print a copy so you can annotate it. It is vital that you read the syllabus very carefully. It will tell you the factual historical knowledge your students need to learn, and the skills they need to develop in order to meet the required assessment objectives.

In this chapter we are going to look at what is contained in a typical syllabus and how you should use it to plan your teaching programme and support your classroom teaching and assessment.

What is in a syllabus?

Different examination boards will have their own way of organising a syllabus; however, a typical syllabus will contain the key areas shown in Figure 5.1.

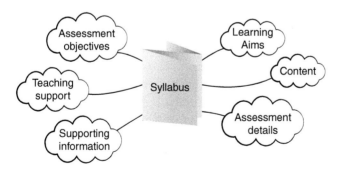

Figure 5.1: The different components of a History syllabus.

5 Approaches to learning and teaching History

1 **Learning aims:** what is the purpose of the course? This is more than just about gaining an understanding of the factual content. What skills and personal attributes should the students develop or enhance through following this course? The aims of a typical History syllabus might include:

- stimulating enthusiasm for learning about the past
- encouraging the development of historical skills, such as analysis, evaluation and communication
- promoting an understanding of key historical concepts
- encouraging international understanding.

2 **Content:** a good syllabus will help you plan your classroom practice by providing the core content and details of optional units. It will provide the key questions that you must ensure your students understand. This will help focus your teaching to prepare your students for the type of questions they might be asked in the final exam.

3 **Assessment details:** this will include information about the number of components in the exam, the different types of question and how many marks are attached to each question. History assessments typically include a mix of short answer questions and longer essays. They often require students to analyse historical sources. These could be primary sources from the time, such as letters, diaries or government reports, or secondary sources written after the period in question, such as books by historians. Your students might need to submit an independent piece of coursework research. Often students are able to devise their own coursework question, on a topic that they are personally interested in.

4 **Assessment objectives:** the syllabus will tell you how each question type is assessed. For example, students might be asked to 'recall, select, organise and deploy knowledge', or 'evaluate a range of sources'.

5 **Teaching support:** the syllabus will tell you what kind of teaching guidance you can expect. You should choose a syllabus that is well supported by sample schemes of work, textbooks and online resources. Example question papers will help you plan your lessons to answer examination questions. Example candidate responses are also very helpful – you should share these with your students using some of the activities described in Chapter 7 **Assessment for Learning**. There may also be details of where you can access teaching guidance to help you prepare your students for the assessment, as well as details of any professional development opportunities. Many examination boards have online forums where you can ask questions and share ideas with fellow teachers at other centres.

6 **Supporting information:** the syllabus should provide practical guidance to help you deliver the course such as, details of how many lessons should be dedicated to each topic, when the examination takes place or how to submit coursework to the exam board for moderation.

What should you study?

Choosing which syllabus to follow can be difficult. A typical syllabus for History will provide a wide choice of topics to study. There will be core content that you have to teach, but also a range of options, offering a choice of different topics and time periods. Courses might focus on different aspects of history, such as military events, political reforms or changes in society. Furthermore, exam boards will set different assessments.

You will need to decide:

- Do I feel that I should teach my students about the history of their own country, or should I expand their knowledge by teaching them about other places?
- Should I pick a syllabus that focuses on topics over a short period of time, or one that asks them to study a longer period? The former may help them develop a great deal of understanding of a short period, but they may not understand the broader context. Conversely, studying a longer period will allow students to develop a sense of how things changed over time, but will provide less depth.
- Should I choose topics that are unfamiliar to my students? This has the benefit of expanding the breadth of their historical knowledge, but may also be a risk because they may find the new material difficult to understand.
- What are the different types of assessment? Are my students well placed to evaluate long pieces of historical writing if that is what is required? If one of the assessment objectives is to evaluate primary sources, how will I teach them the skills to do so?
- If there is a requirement to complete coursework, does my school have the resources (such as access to historical research) to enable them to carry out independent research for the coursework? If I allow students to decide what they would like to research for their coursework, I must be able to provide them with access to suitable materials.

Teacher Tip

Coursework often asks students to undertake some research beyond the course textbook. This can be difficult if your school library is not well stocked with history books. Try contacting local universities to see if you can arrange access for your students to their more extensive libraries. Your students may be able to go to the library and use the resources there.

Skills versus knowledge

The syllabus will tell you:

- what knowledge (such as key events, individuals and dates) your students need to gain
- what skills they need to evidence when writing their exam answers.

Historians debate the balance between skills and knowledge: which one is more important? Some historians argue that mastery of the factual detail comes first: students need to know what happened before they can analyse events and reach their own judgement. Others see History as a vehicle for developing transferable skills, such as analysis, writing and weighing up both sides of an argument. Both viewpoints have merit. The syllabus may give you a percentage 'weighting' that shows how many marks are available to students for showing mastery of factual details, and how many for evidencing skills, such as analysing sources. Read this carefully and use it to make sure that you provide your students with a good balance of skills and factual content.

Selecting resources

Once you have read the syllabus and identified the historical content and skills your students need to grasp, you will need to find resources to help support their learning in the classroom. Many History teachers are making increasing use of online resources in their teaching, given the tremendous array of materials available. However, even the most experienced teachers will make full use of high-quality textbooks to provide a firm foundation of content and activities for their students. Since such a wide range of books is available, how should you set about choosing a suitable textbook?

Here are some issues to consider:

- If relevant, look at textbooks which meet the needs of the examination syllabus you are following. They will help you prepare for the assessment requirements of the course.
- A good textbook will provide sufficient depth of historical content in its coverage of events. In particular, there should be a wide range of stimulating primary and secondary source material.
- Are key terms laid out clearly and explained? This is important in building a truly inclusive classroom and will be particularly helpful in supporting the needs of EAL students.
- Is the subject content linked to stimulating activities which provide an exploratory approach to learning?
- Does the textbook have accompanying electronic resources?
- Will the textbook encourage students to review and reflect on their learning?

In short, a well-chosen textbook should help to enhance your teaching and provide students with an appropriate range of support and extension opportunities to meet the needs of all.

Some textbooks may be accompanied with support materials which are available as a CD-ROM or through the publisher's website. These additional resources can often prove especially helpful to new teachers or those teaching a new course. Supplementary materials, such as those linked to this book, will give you a framework to apply new ideas in the classroom.

Alongside the textbook, you will want to use additional material to reflect the diverse needs of your students. Course books have to be written well in advance of their publication date, so you might want to add some more up-to-date material to your lessons, linking the historical period to more contemporary events. Alongside books there are now many websites offering resources, such as PowerPoints, worksheets and even entire lesson plans. If these require a subscription, check that they are age- and skill-level-appropriate before you subscribe.

Teacher Tip

You can create supplementary resources yourself. This is time-consuming and perhaps only worthwhile if you can reuse them over several years. However, since you best know the ability level and characteristics of your students, it is a good way of ensuring that your resources are accessible and valuable.

Planning your teaching

The syllabus will provide a basic framework that tells you what you need to teach, but it will not tell you how to do so. Once you have read the syllabus, you will need to plan how to deliver the material and the skills that it requires, breaking down the syllabus into individual lessons. I construct a scheme of work: a plan of lessons that will enable me to deliver the content required by the syllabus. I break this down into a weekly plan, and then break the weekly plan down further, into individual lesson plans (Figure 5.2). This includes suggested classroom activities, homework tasks and resources to use.

Figure 5.2: This diagram shows the process of planning your teaching, from the broad curriculum down to your individual lesson plans.

The Example Lesson Plan (online) is the first lesson of a scheme of work about Civil Rights in the United States. The key questions are taken directly from the syllabus. The lesson plan lists specific activities that cover content on the syllabus. It also contains a range of questions of varying difficulty both to support less confident students and to challenge students who are moving faster through the material. It includes links to PowerPoints and video clips so that you can access them easily in lessons. It reminds you what homework to set so that you can start the following lesson with a discussion about what students have learned.

The lesson begins with a discussion of the nature of Civil Rights, to ensure that students have a sound understanding before they begin their study of the specific country and period in question. It then gives students a very broad overview of the key events in the lives of the four different minority groups – women, Native Americans, African Americans, and workers and trade unions. It enables students to make some initial judgements by assessing and comparing the level of progress each group made towards achieving equality in Civil Rights.

Key points to reflect upon when writing a scheme of work

- Be prepared to change your scheme of work. Having a plan does not mean that you should stick to it rigidly. You may find your class needs more or less time on something; you will only know this after you have got to know them.
- Allow time in your scheme of work not only to teach the factual content of the course but also to practise skills like essay writing and source analysis.
- How much material can you set students to learn for homework? The more factual detail that they can learn outside of class, the more time you will have for engaging activities in your lessons. See Chapter 6 **Active learning** for ideas.
- Make sure you have a range of different activities to keep up the interest level of the students. See Chapter 8 **Metacognition** for advice on the different ways in which students learn.
- Consider ways in which you will assess learning, and write them into the scheme.
- Include differentiated activities in your scheme so you can support the diverse needs of students.
- If the syllabus includes coursework, plan carefully how you will deliver this, building time into your teaching to meet students to discuss their work and support their research.
- The syllabus will tell you how many marks are allocated to the different assessment objectives: ensure that your scheme of work allocates sufficient time to each objective.
- The pace with which you cover the material is important. If you do not cover enough in the first part of the year, your teaching will be

rushed later on. However, in my experience it is best to start with a slow pace, giving time for your students to become confident in the material. If they do not gain a good grasp of the material early in the course, they may become disillusioned, particularly when they encounter more difficult material later.

☑ LESSON IDEA ONLINE 5.1: EVALUATING HISTORICAL INTERPRETATIONS

Analysing historians' interpretations is a key skill in many syllabuses for History. Use this lesson idea to help students understand how to analyse and evaluate different historians' interpretations and to decide which interpretation they find the most convincing.

☑ LESSON IDEA ONLINE 5.2: ANALYSING AND EVALUATING PRIMARY SOURCES

Another key skill is evaluating primary historical sources. Use this lesson idea to help students understand how to analyse and evaluate primary sources.

Teacher Tip

You will need to be flexible in the use of your scheme of work. However well you plan, there will always be unforeseen events that impact upon your teaching. Think about these situations and how you would alter your teaching to accommodate them:

- An event in the morning's news is relevant to the historical topic your class is studying. Students are interested and want to discuss the event. You are keen to encourage this enthusiastic engagement, but it leaves you less time to cover the content of the lesson.
- You have a number of very confident students in your class, and they always complete the activities much faster than other members of the group.
- There was a fire alarm and your whole lesson had to be cancelled.

Teaching beyond the exam requirements

Obviously, it is essential to address the requirements of the examination syllabus. However, it is also important for you to extend your students' understanding beyond that required to pass the exam. Teaching students only to succeed in the exam can lead to very dull lessons. While it is vital that your students understand success criteria and assessment objectives, their long-term interest in History will only be engaged when you take the time to discuss the fascinating events and figures that make History such an exciting subject. This is true whether knowing about them is required to pass the exam or not. Ultimately, an interested, engaged student who enjoys their historical studies will learn more effectively, revise more conscientiously and be more likely to succeed.

Summary

In this chapter, we have discussed the following considerations:

- Make sure that you have read the syllabus very carefully – you should use it to plan your teaching.

- If the syllabus gives you a range of topics to choose from, consider what your students will enjoy learning about and how well placed you are to deliver the course successfully.

- The syllabus will provide detail of the historical content that your students must know and the skills they must develop – plan your scheme of work to ensure you deliver this material.

- Similarly, it will tell you what assessment objectives your students must address to ensure success in their course – make sure you leave enough time in your scheme of work to practise meeting these objectives.

6 | Active learning

What is active learning?

Active learning is a pedagogical practice that places student learning at its centre. It focuses on *how* students learn, not just on *what* they learn. We as teachers need to encourage students to 'think hard', rather than passively receive information. Active learning encourages students to take responsibility for their learning and supports them in becoming independent and confident learners in school and beyond.

Research shows us that it is not possible to transmit understanding to students by simply telling them what they need to know. Instead, we need to make sure that we challenge students' thinking and support them in building their own understanding. Active learning encourages more complex thought processes, such as evaluating, analysing and synthesising, which foster a greater number of neural connections in the brain. While some students may be able to create their own meaning from information received passively, others will not. Active learning enables all students to build knowledge and understanding in response to the opportunities we provide.

Why adopt an active learning approach?

We can enrich all areas of the curriculum, at all stages, by embedding an active learning approach.

In active learning, we need to think not only about the content but also about the process. It gives students greater involvement and control over their learning. This encourages all students to stay focused on their learning, which will often give them greater enthusiasm for their studies. Active learning is intellectually stimulating and taking this approach encourages a level of academic discussion with our students that we, as teachers, can also enjoy. Healthy discussion means that students are engaging with us as a partner in their learning.

Students will better be able to revise for examinations in the sense that revision really is 're-vision' of the ideas that they already understand.

Active learning develops students' analytical skills, supporting them to be better problem solvers and more effective in their application of knowledge. They will be prepared to deal with challenging and unexpected situations. As a result, students are more confident in continuing to learn once they have left school and are better equipped for the transition to higher education and the workplace.

What are the challenges of incorporating active learning?

When people start thinking about putting active learning into practice, they often make the mistake of thinking more about the activity they want to design than about the learning. The most important thing is to put the student and the learning at the centre of our planning. A task can be quite simple but still get the student to think critically and independently. Sometimes a complicated task does not actually help to develop the student's thinking or understanding at all. We need to consider carefully what we want our students to learn or understand and then shape the task to activate this learning.

Active learning and the History curriculum

History is often viewed as a very content-heavy subject, requiring the memorisation of lots of facts and dates. Although these can be taught in an instructive way, with you telling students what they need to know, a deeper understanding can be developed by engaging students' thought processes through a wide range of stimuli. Ask yourself:

- How can I make sure I challenge my students' thinking rather than simply presenting them with facts?
- Can I present factual historical detail to students in a range of different formats? How can I encourage students to be engaged through visual imagery, auditory stimulus or debate and conversation with each other?
- How can I encourage students to become active participants and take greater responsibility for their learning, relying less on my factual knowledge so that they develop the independent skills needed for success when they leave school?

LESSON IDEA ONLINE 6.1: STIMULATING INITIAL INTEREST

Students learn at a deeper level when they are curious about the subject. Active learning strategies can encourage this. Use this lesson idea to stimulate students' interest and enthusiasm for the subject.

LESSON IDEA 6.2: DEVELOPING STUDENTS' ANALYTICAL SKILLS AND MAKING EFFECTIVE USE OF THEORY

Students learn actively through undertaking an investigation or enquiry. Instead of giving them a topic to study, give them a question to research such as 'Why did William win the Battle of Hastings?' or 'How successful were the Suffragettes in Britain?' They might find this daunting at first because they do not possess the research skills required. You might ask them to watch a movie and start the lesson by discussing how accurate they thought the movie was. This could lead into a wider debate on the value and problems

→

of movies claiming to represent historical events. This will stimulate further engagement: understanding that the study of History can involve debates relevant to today will further their interest in the subject.

Teacher Tip

You may need to direct students towards reliable internet sites. Research of this kind can provide an opportunity to teach students to critically evaluate where they find information, an essential skill for a historian. They should think about internet sites in the same way as they would any other source of information, asking questions such as 'Who wrote the website?' and 'What was their motivation for creating the website?'

Active learning strategies

There may be times, particularly when introducing an enquiry, that you will need to talk to the whole class about the topic. For example, you might begin your lesson with a PowerPoint presentation outlining the topic to be covered. However, delivering a long lecture to students is rarely effective because students become passive listeners rather than taking an active involvement in their learning. Furthermore, it is not possible for you to assess the quality of their learning.

So once you have decided that you will not simply 'tell' students about a historical topic, you will need to create activities that help them to learn. This is your chance to be creative! Active learning strategies work best when students transform information into a different form; for example, taking written text and turning it into a poster. Work is best undertaken collaboratively: now that they are less reliant on you, students will need to support each other. Figure 6.1 provides a few examples of active learning strategies.

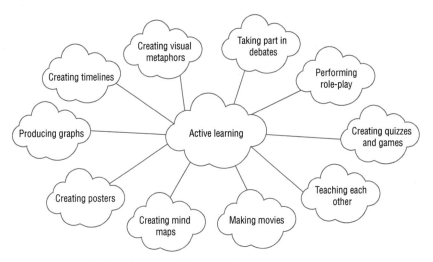

Figure 6.1: Active learning strategies.

Creating visual metaphors

⌨ LESSON IDEA ONLINE 6.3: USING VISUAL METAPHORS TO EXPLORE CAUSATION

Use this lesson idea to include visual metaphors to help plan an essay.

Taking part in debates

A really active way to engage students is to ask them to debate a key question. Debates enable students to work collaboratively, listening to a diverse range of perspectives and synthesising them to create their own personal judgement.

LESSON IDEA 6.4: ENCOURAGING STUDENTS TO DEBATE

Give your students a proposition, for example: 'The actions of individual leaders were the most important reason for the collapse of Apartheid.' How far do you agree with this statement? →

Split the group in half, with one side speaking in favour of the proposition and the other against. You must give students plenty of time to develop their arguments. Some students may not want to speak, so encourage them as follows: each student is given three sweets; each time they make a contribution to the debate they are allowed to eat a sweet; they are not allowed to have one if they do not contribute. Not only does this encourage those less confident to contribute, but it prevents any one student from dominating the debate: once they have had all three sweets, they are not allowed to contribute again.

Performing role-play

Role-play is a very enjoyable way in which students can learn about historical events. Role-playing scenes from history can be a helpful way of reinforcing and checking students' understanding of key events. If following complex text is challenging, turning that text into a visual medium can help students.

LESSON IDEA 6.5: HISTORICAL ROLE-PLAY

Give each student a narrative of a key event to read before the lesson. Then give them key figures to act out, writing a script and turning the narrative into a play that is performed for the class. If there is a historical question to debate such as 'Should King Charles I of England have been executed?' or 'Was the Treaty of Versailles to harsh on Germany?' You could use a trial format: One side acts as the defence and the other as the prosecution who can present pieces of evidence or witnesses to the court. A third group of students acts as the jury who listen to the evidence presented to them. At the end of the lesson the jury decide which argument they find most persuasive.

Creating quizzes and games

Playing games is a fun way to encourage students. Use games such as quizzes in teams, crosswords, Pictionary or word searches at the start of a lesson as a quick way of testing students' understanding of the homework. This allows you to correct any misconceptions before further work is completed. Similarly, they make excellent ways to test learning at the end of lessons and to identify those students who have struggled to grasp key details.

Teacher Tip

Asking students to make their own quiz questions or games to test the learning of their peers is a creative and effective way to encourage them to learn. These quizzes can save you work in the future: they can be used as a recap at the start of the next lesson.

Teaching each other

Remember that engaged and interested students can be a very valuable teaching resource; asking them to teach each other can be a rewarding way of achieving this. Describing their research orally to their peers in a way that their audience can understand also requires students to use higher order thinking.

LESSON IDEA 6.6: PEER TEACHING

Ask students to undertake a research task and then teach their peers what they have discovered during their investigation. The students will really need to master the subject if they are going to teach someone else about it. Once they have been taught by their peers, you could ask students to explain what they have learned to the class, or use a short assessment task, such as a quiz, to check that they have been taught correctly.

Making movies

New technology such as smartphones and tablets have made making movies in class a very accessible, quick and effective learning activity. Students could write and record a historical scene – perhaps a famous trial or political meeting – or they could record a debate where different groups argue for and against a statement.

Creating mind maps

A mind map is a diagram that visually shows the relationships between different factors. Students start by writing the key question or concept in the centre of the page. For example, 'The most important reason that British women won the vote in 1918 was the First World War'. Students then organise a range of other reasons, noting evidence for them being an important factor around these key points (Figure 6.2). There are websites that can help you produce mind maps.

Figure 6.2: Mind map showing challenges facing India after Independence in 1947.

Creating posters

Asking students to turn text into visual imagery is a very useful way of checking how far they have grasped the key points of your lesson. This lesson works particularly well if students are asked to create their own version of actual posters. For example, to create a poster publicising a political party, spreading propaganda, advertising a product such as a new invention or medical breakthrough, or recruiting soldiers for war.

Producing graphs

Creating a graph to chart changes can help students to visualise the patterns of historical change and development. Graphs can show chronological development and also the impact of key events. For example, a graph could show patterns of immigration into a country but also mark the impact of events that might reduce or increase immigration such as wars or changes in legal restrictions.

Making timelines

Placing key events into chronological order can be very helpful in understanding why an event took place when it did. Using different colour coding to mark key points, such as wars, increased or reduced political control, the impact of economic developments, can add an easy to understand level of sophistication.

The role of the teacher

It is important to acknowledge that using active learning strategies fundamentally changes the role of a teacher. Instead of so-called 'teacher-centred' learning, you will act as the students' guide.

However, learning in this way is not the same as undirected or unstructured learning. It is not entirely independent and you still play a vital though very different role. You will need to do the following:

- Ensure students know the overall purpose of the lesson. This may require communicating some instructions, objectives, success criteria and key concepts before students branch off into activities.
- Find ways to 'flip' learning by creating or providing books, articles or websites that students of all ability levels can learn from before the lesson, so they can all come to the lesson prepared to apply higher order thinking. This requires very careful thought: students should receive directions on what to research, such as the answer to a particular question. If students do not receive enough direction, their research can become undirected and lack clear purpose.

- Help create a supportive and collaborative learning environment. If your students are going to feel confident and comfortable in sharing and being creative, you must set the behavioural guidelines and expectations that ensure that other students listen and share in a supportive and non-confrontational manner. An active learning environment is one that encourages students to take risks and make their own judgements; you must ensure that they feel comfortable to do so. When students are fearful or feel under duress, they will not learn effectively.
- Create engaging learning activities that stimulate students' interest. Students learn actively when they are engaging with material, perhaps by transforming it into a new medium. This requires very careful planning.
- Think on your feet: when you ask students to be creative, you will sometimes be surprised by what they come up with! This can be daunting, but the value to their learning is worth the risk.
- Be aware of the learning needs of all members of the class. You will need to create active learning strategies that meet differentiated needs. There is more detail in Chapter 10 **Inclusive education**.
- Centre the lesson on sound subject matter. You must possess the knowledge to be able to correct any misconceptions or factual errors.
- Check students' work in order to guide all members of the class to successful outcomes. You will need to build in opportunities to assess the progress and understanding of students during lessons. There is more detail in Chapter 7 **Assessment for Learning**.

▣ LESSON IDEA ONLINE 6.7: FACILITATING ACTIVE LEARNING

Use this lesson to encourage students to discuss, debate, question and analyse.

Collaboration in the History classroom

Collaboration is a vital aspect of active learning. Instead of simply listening to you, students will be sharing their ideas with each other. You will need to think about the layout of the classroom to help with this:

students need to be able to share ideas with their peers as well as listen to instruction from you.

Some students find it hard to share their ideas. Careful thought will need to go into which students work together, how you expect them to work and how you will communicate this clearly to them.

Teacher Tip

Think about:

- Which students might intimidate others?
- Which ones are good listeners and could support the learning of quieter or less confident students?
- Which ones are secure in their knowledge and able to communicate it well to less able students?

Grouping is vital: with less direction from you, students must feel supported by their peers.

Learning outside the classroom

Students can also learn actively outside of the classroom. A key part of active learning is to give them a greater sense of ownership of their learning. They could be encouraged to visit a museum, art gallery or site of historical interest to undertake a research project. Having an emotional involvement in a topic helps engage students. They might interview a family member who remembers a historical event or, better still, was present at the actual event itself. When students empathise and become emotionally invested, they see greater value and relevance in what they are studying. They become more interested and engaged.

Teacher Tip

Continuing professional development emphasises that learning for teachers, as well as for our students, is an ongoing process directed at improving the quality of teaching and learning. This is often achieved through encouraging innovation and collaboration. Accessing different sources of expertise within your own school or on a wider local or national level will benefit your teaching. Developing a community of professional learners within your school can give you the opportunity to share good practice and explore approaches to teaching within and across different subject areas.

Summary

In this chapter we have discussed the following:

- Active learning gives students greater opportunities to engage with historical facts in a creative way, to make History lessons enjoyable. When students find learning fun, they learn at a deeper and more effective level.

- Active learning helps students to become more independent and less reliant on you, and to develop higher order transferable skills.

- Students will need to collaborate with their peers and support each other's learning.

- You have a vital role in guiding students through the learning tasks, setting clear objectives and correcting any misunderstanding and misconceptions.

Assessment
for Learning

7

What is Assessment for Learning?

Assessment for Learning (AfL) is a teaching approach that generates feedback that can be used to improve students' performance. Students become more involved in the learning process and, from this, gain confidence in what they are expected to learn and to what standard. We as teachers gain insights into a student's level of understanding of a particular concept or topic, which helps to inform how we support their progression.

We need to understand the meaning and method of giving purposeful feedback to optimise learning. Feedback can be informal, such as oral comments to help students think through problems, or formal, such as the use of rubrics to help clarify and scaffold learning and assessment objectives.

Why use Assessment for Learning?

By following well-designed approaches to AfL, we can understand better how our students are learning and use this to plan what we will do next with a class or individual students (see Figure 7.1). We can help our students to see what they are aiming for and to understand what they need to do to get there. AfL makes learning visible; it helps students understand more accurately the nature of the material they are learning and themselves as learners. The quality of interactions and feedback between students and teachers becomes critical to the learning process.

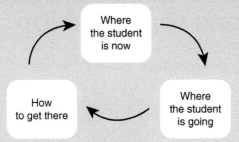

Figure 7.1: How can we use this plan to help our students?

We can use AfL to help our students focus on specific elements of their learning and to take greater responsibility for how they might move forward. AfL creates a valuable connection between assessment and learning activities, as the clarification of objectives will have a direct impact on how we devise teaching and learning strategies. AfL techniques can support students in becoming more confident in what they are learning, reflective in how they are learning, more likely to try out new approaches, and more engaged in what they are being asked to learn.

What are the challenges of incorporating AfL?

The use of AfL does not mean that we need to test students more frequently. It would be easy to just increase the amount of summative assessment and use this formatively as a regular method of helping us decide what to do next in our teaching. We can judge how much learning has taken place through ways other than testing, including, above all, communicating with our students in a variety of ways and getting to know them better as individuals.

Questions for reflection

As reflective professionals, it is always valuable to reflect upon our practice. Assessment is one of the most time-consuming roles that we undertake as teachers, so it is worth asking yourself how effectively you are using assessment. Think about the following:

- How can I help my students make the most of the feedback that we provide them, encouraging them to look beyond the grade they have received and to engage with the written feedback?
- How can my feedback help students to reflect upon their progress and to explicitly identify what they need to do to improve their work?
- How can I prevent students from getting the same grade time and again and becoming demotivated?
- How can I ensure that students understand the criteria for success in the assessments that I set?

Key aspects of Assessment for Learning

AfL addresses all the above issues. Here are some of the key aspects of successful AfL:

- It is Assessment *for* Learning, *not* Assessment *of* Learning, because students are equipped with detailed knowledge of the target criteria as well as specific feedback to understand how to meet them.
- It should allow students immediate opportunities to act upon feedback.
- It de-emphasises the importance of the grade and instead helps to develop the resilience and thinking skills necessary to be a lifelong, independent learner.
- Assessment may take a wide range of forms. You should be assessing learning not only through written tests, but also through evaluating a student's contributions to debates, one-to-one discussions, presentations and so on.

- The assessment of student progress should enable you to alter your teaching to address their specific needs.
- It is ongoing, throughout the course, not at the end as with summative assessment.

AfL has been shown to be one of the most effective strategies in supporting student progress in both the short and long term. As eminent educationalist Shirley Clarke writes:

> Formative Assessment [or Assessment for Learning as it has become known] is about the involvement of students in the learning process, beyond anything traditional teaching has previously allowed. The proven effect of teaching in this way is that students do BETTER than before and become life-long independent learners.

Shirley Clarke (*Formative Assessment in the Secondary Classroom*, Hodder Education, London, 2005).

Teacher Tip

There is a wealth of research literature about AfL. The most influential of these is *Black Box: Raising Standards Through Classroom Assessment* by Paul Black and Dylan Wiliam of King's College, University of London. Why not download their study from the internet and choose one new strategy to use with your students? If after reflection you feel it was not effective, think about how you might alter it to better support your class.

Using questioning in the classroom

Using AfL means that questioning should be used not to simply confirm that students have remembered key facts, to make shy students talk or to check they have been listening. You can use questions to encourage students to reflect upon their learning and to enable you to assess students' progress. You can then alter their lesson plans accordingly to meet their specific needs.

Imagine that you are teaching your class about the victory of Mao Zedong's Communist Party in the Chinese Civil War. Examples of questions that do not encourage students to reflect deeply might be:

1 When did the Chinese Civil War end?
2 Where did Mao announce his victory in the Civil War?
3 Who can tell me exactly how many soldiers died in the Civil War?

These questions are 'closed'. Either students remember them, or they do not. Even if the students answer them correctly, they are not empowered to answer further questions better. Moreover, you will not know whether students could apply this knowledge to answer questions other than these specific ones. More helpful 'higher order' questions to ask would be:

1 What does the result of the Chinese Civil War tell us about support for the Communist Party?
2 Is it always true that the most popular party will succeed?
3 How would you explain why Mao was victorious?
4 What questions would you need to ask in order to explain why Mao and the Communists won the Chinese Civil War?

There are many ways of questioning students without making them feel uncomfortable. For example, for short-answer or multiple-choice questions you could use whiteboards: ask students a question to which they write an answer and hold it up. This is a non-threatening way of checking who is making progress and who might benefit from additional support. If students feel nervous and are tempted to copy the answer of peers that they perceive as more knowledgeable, simply ask them to close their eyes while writing their answer. Remember to give students lots of time to answer questions: the pressure on teachers to get through the course often leads them to become impatient, but it is important that students have time to reflect upon what they have learned before answering.

Checking students' understanding

Students may not feel confident to confess that they do not understand the topic that they have been studying. Even if you ask 'Does everyone understand?', they may be reluctant to admit that they are struggling and not answer. Alternatively, they might not understand, but answer 'yes' because they mistakenly believe that they do. Either way, you will not receive accurate information about the progress of your students. You will continue on with the next topic, believing that the whole class has grasped the previous topic. Their lack of understanding may well not be revealed until a summative assessment, possibly the final exam. It is vital that you do not allow this to happen.

LESSON IDEA 7.1: USING VISUAL METAPHORS

Use mini whiteboards to confirm that students have understood key content. Ask them to convert written material, perhaps something that they have read for homework, into a visual metaphor (Figure 7.2). Give them only a short amount of time to do this. Once they have done so, they should show their work to a peer and ask them to explain what has been drawn. The process of turning written text into a picture tests students' ability to reflect upon what they have learned and distil it into a simple medium.

Figure 7.2

If any students have drawn an image that does not help answer the question, you will be able to identify them and offer support.

Teacher Tip

Use a 'traffic lights' activity to encourage students to reflect upon their progress. Give them a list of the key points of the course, and ask them to grade the points according to three colours: Red if they are not feeling confident, Amber if they are moderately confident and Green for very confident. Use language such as 'How confident are you?' because it is less threatening and students are more likely to give you an honest answer. Collect the answers at different stages of the topic: if you do this regularly, you can use this information to adjust your teaching.

Ensuring that students can understand and apply success criteria

Students need to be able to understand the success criteria for the task they are doing. For example, if they understand exactly what makes for a successful essay, they will be able to identify what they did well and what they need to do to improve. They will be better able to understand the advice you have given them in your feedback, and will be able to match up their essay against the criteria to generate targets for improvement.

LESSON IDEA 7.2: UNDERSTANDING AND APPLYING SUCCESS CRITERIA

Prepare two answers to a specific exam question, one top level and another with weaknesses. Ask students to read the mark scheme for the question and discuss exactly what is required for each grade or level. Start by showing students the weak answer, but do not let them know that it is a poor response. Ask the students to imagine that they are an examiner and to use the mark scheme to read and mark the answer, annotating the positives and negatives of the response and then discussing what they thought of the answer to ensure their understanding of the criteria for success. Repeat the exercise with the better answer; again end with a discussion that ensures that students are clear as to why this answer would be more successful.

☑ **LESSON IDEA ONLINE 7.3: SELECTING EVIDENCE**
Use this lesson idea to help develop students' understanding of
how to identify and categorise historical evidence in order to
answer questions successfully.

Effective feedback

It is vital to provide students with timely feedback that helps them to
see what they did well, as well as what they should work on to improve
in future assessments. Feedback should be very specific and provide
advice on how to progress. Unlike Science or Maths questions, History
essays ask students to provide a lengthy written interpretation that
must be read closely to ascertain how far it has met the success criteria.
As this requires a considerable amount of time, feedback should be as
effective as possible to enable students to improve. Try to avoid vague
comments such as 'poor communication', 'you have misunderstood' or
even 'well done'. These do not help students identify how to improve: in
what way is their argument poorly communicated? What exactly have
they misunderstood? What have they done well? Feedback must help
students understand what is good or bad about their work and enable
them to set their own targets for improvement.

Here are examples of unhelpful feedback:

1 This is very nicely written.
2 I agree with your overall argument.
3 This is a very enjoyable essay.
4 This is very well presented.
5 I am impressed with the amount that you have written in the time
   limit: well done!

None of these examples of feedback would advance the skills of
students to enable them to answer further questions: some of them
might make the student happy for a few minutes, but they would not

be better placed to answer different or more difficult questions in the future. Examples of more effective feedback are:

1 This is nicely written but tells the story, rather than providing analysis. Check the mark criteria again – what does it say about the need to apply skills such as analysis or evaluation?
2 Your overall argument is compelling, but in paragraph 2 you failed to apply sufficient factual knowledge, such as statistics or dates, to support your otherwise convincing argument. Return to your notes on this topic and rewrite this paragraph, ensuring that you add at least two more pieces of pertinent factual detail.

The latter point here is important: it is essential that students are given timely opportunities to apply your feedback. Too often the class will have moved on to new topics or new types of questions and they will not have had the chance to use your feedback to improve. If this is the case, the effectiveness of the feedback will be greatly decreased.

Teacher Tip

Oral feedback is a good alternative to written comments because it is more personalised; evidence shows that this sense of personalisation can be a strong motivating factor for students. There is a range of software available that can help you record your feedback so that students can listen to it and also save it for future reference.

Given the pressures upon teachers to ensure that all content in a course is completed, it is very easy for feedback of assessed work to become an afterthought, perhaps with essays given back at the end of the lesson and students told to read your comments in their own time. With the time pressures that students are themselves under, this will probably lead to a superficial glance at their grade and little engagement with your comments or reflection upon how to meet success criteria. Instead, make sure you give students plenty of time to read your comments. Build time into your lessons for students to note their positives and also identify targets for improvement. This will be time well spent.

Peer assessment

Peer assessment has been shown to be a hugely effective strategy to improve student outcomes. Students learn a great deal from assessing others' work. Marking their peers' work by using the assessment criteria compels students to actively engage with these criteria and to develop a detailed understanding of what is required. This then helps them when they write future assessments.

Figure 7.3

There are some important points to consider when using peer assessment:

- Students must feel able to discuss each other's work in a positive and unthreatening environment; it is your role to ensure that this atmosphere is created.
- Remember that some students may feel insecure about having a peer read their work.
- Feedback should always be constructive and should not seek to humiliate or embarrass. Again, a good understanding of the assessment criteria will help students to write comments that use the language of the criteria; this will avoid their comments being too personalised or judgemental.

You might start by writing a sample paragraph or using work from a previous year group to help students get used to applying the criteria.

Students must feel that it is beneficial to receive feedback from their peers and to read the work of other members of the class. They should see assessments as part of a long-term learning process, and feedback as an opportunity to reflect, discuss and collaborate. You should model this behaviour to your students, using positive language as well as constructive criticism as appropriate.

Teacher Tip

Make sure that you set some ground rules for peer assessment. Students must be taught to provide constructive criticism that is based entirely upon the mark scheme, and avoid any personal comments that might be interpreted as hurtful or abusive.

The role of the teacher

Advocates of a traditional form of assessment are sometimes worried that peer assessment devalues the role of the teacher. This is a misconception: the teacher plays a critical role. It is you who makes clear the expectations for peer assessment, you who will provide model answers to enhance the understanding of success criteria and you who will help change the expectation that the teacher is an 'expert' transferring knowledge to passive students, in a situation where a 'learning dialogue' takes place between teacher and learner. Students must understand not only what they are learning, but also why they are doing so and how they can improve.

Adopting an AfL approach can be daunting. A key aspect is to ensure that students take note of your feedback and act upon it. Very often students will only look at the final mark that you give them and not address the more important point of the assessment, namely what they should do next time. To avoid this, you might try not actually putting a mark on the assessment. You can still record a mark in your mark book or results spreadsheet so you can chart their progress.

Students may be accustomed to receiving a grade on their work, and you will need to explain why you are providing formative comments instead. It may take time for students to become used to this. You might offer to show the students their marks, but only after they have gone through some of the AfL lesson ideas in this chapter. Students will quickly see that using strategies such as peer assessment or discussing success criteria are much more helpful than simply seeing a score written on their work. Take time to let other teachers know what you are doing, sharing good practice and explaining the benefits to them. Let parents know that research shows that this approach is beneficial to students. Once they see the value in focusing on formative feedback rather than the final mark, students usually stop asking for their grade.

Students' engagement with their own learning is a vital aspect of AfL. Instead of giving students their targets for improvement, ask them to use your feedback and reflect on their progress to identify targets for improvement the next time that they are writing a similar essay. They should write these down and put them with their class notes.

Teacher Tip

When you set students their next assessment, ask them to read back over the targets for improvement. Ask them to identify one target and to write it at the top of the page the next time they write an assessment. This is to act as a reminder that this is their priority to address. At the end of the test, allow the students time to highlight in their essay where they think they have met their goal. When reading the assessment, it will be easy to check whether or not they have done so or not.

Summary

In this chapter we have discussed:

- Assessment for Learning is different from Assessment of Learning. It is the use of formative assessment to help students reflect upon their progress and to identify what they need to do to improve their work.

- Asking the right kinds of questions of the students is critical to assessing learning.

- Checking students' understanding of a topic throughout their course of lessons will allow you to adjust your teaching to support their individual needs.

- It is vital that students understand the success criteria for any task or assessment.

- Peer assessment is a key aspect of AfL.

- As a teacher, try to encourage an ethos in the classroom that sees assessment as a process, that helps students to improve.

Metacognition

8

What is metacognition?

Metacognition describes the processes involved when students plan, monitor, evaluate and make changes to their own learning behaviours. These processes help students to think about their own learning more explicitly and ensure that they are able to meet a learning goal that they have identified themselves or that we, as teachers, have set.

Metacognitive learners recognise what they find easy or difficult. They understand the demands of a particular learning task and are able to identify different approaches they could use to tackle a problem. Metacognitive learners are also able to make adjustments to their learning as they monitor their progress towards a particular learning goal.

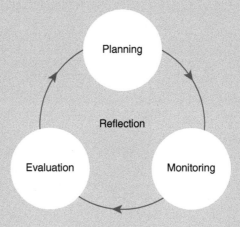

Figure 8.1: A helpful way to think about the phases involved in metacognition.

During the *planning* phase, students think about the explicit learning goal we have set and what we are asking them to do. As teachers, we need to make clear to students what success looks like in any given task before they embark on it. Students build on their prior knowledge, reflect on strategies they have used before and consider how they will approach the new task.

As students put their plan into action, they are constantly *monitoring* the progress they are making towards their learning goal. If the strategies they had decided to use are not working, they may decide to try something different.

Once they have completed the task, students determine how successful the strategy they used was in helping them to achieve their learning goal. During this *evaluation* phase, students think about what went well and what didn't go as well to help them decide what they could do differently next time. They may also think about what other types of problems they could solve using the same strategy.

Reflection is a fundamental part of the plan–monitor–evaluate process and there are various ways in which we can support our students to reflect on their learning process. In order to apply a metacognitive approach, students need access to a set of strategies that they can use and a classroom environment that encourages them to explore and develop their metacognitive skills.

Why teach metacognitive skills?

Research evidence suggests that the use of metacognitive skills plays an important role in successful learning. Metacognitive practices help students to monitor their own progress and take control of their learning. Metacognitive learners think about and learn from their mistakes and modify their learning strategies accordingly. Students who use metacognitive techniques find it improves their academic achievement across subjects, as it helps them transfer what they have learnt from one context to another context, or from a previous task to a new task.

What are the challenges of developing students' metacognitive skills?

For metacognition to be commonplace in the classroom, we need to encourage students to take time to think about and learn from their mistakes. Many students are afraid to make mistakes, meaning that they are less likely to take risks, explore new ways of thinking or tackle unfamiliar problems. We as teachers are instrumental in shaping the culture of learning in a classroom. For metacognitive practices to thrive, students need to feel confident enough to make mistakes, to discuss their mistakes and ultimately to view them as valuable, and often necessary, learning opportunities.

How can metacognition help History students?

Awareness of metacognition can help History students:

- identify for themselves the best way to learn the many factual details that they are required to remember
- successfully plan different types of essay questions, identifying strategies that work for them and also ways that are less helpful
- identify and utilise different strategies to help comprehend the wide range of detailed reading, including competing historical interpretations, required for the successful study of History.

How can you help students to develop metacognition?

Students will not automatically develop metacognition. You can help them to develop their awareness by acting as a role model. Talk to your students about how you learn and what strategies you use to master new materials. How do you learn new factual material when preparing to teach a topic that you have not taught before? How do you undertake research? What strategies do you use to remember the key dates of a historical period? How do you react when you find this process difficult, and what adjustments do you make? Ensure that your students know that learning is a process that requires reflection and perseverance, whatever your age or educational stage.

Employing teaching approaches that encourage students to reflect on what kind of strategy they should employ to evaluate historical evidence will help them to get used to a metacognitive approach.

📝 **LESSON IDEA ONLINE 8.1: CREATING 'CRITERIA' TO MAKE DEVELOPED JUDGEMENTS**

Use this lesson idea to encourage students to identify the criteria that they can use to study historical figures or events. The lesson uses the modernisation of Vietnam as an example, but the approach can be transferred to other historical topics.

Teacher Tip

Students who are very focused upon their personal examination success are sometimes unable to see the long-term benefits of developing metacognition. You could invite someone who has been successful in their career – perhaps an entrepreneur, politician, author or artist – to come to the school and talk to students about how the techniques and attitudes that they learned in school helped them to succeed.

Learning preferences

Encourage students to reflect upon how they learn and to recognise what strategies work best for them. Some students find it useful to look at visual images: a student studying the success of Stalin's cult of personality might, for example, find it valuable to examine propaganda posters (Figure 8.2) or watch newsreels from the time. Other students learn best from tactile interactions: a lesson that asked them to identify the causes of the Great Depression might feature a card-sort of different factors, with students physically moving them into a rank order. Listening to a teacher talk about a topic can be another way students learn. Students aware of their metacognitive processes will be able to reflect upon which style of learning they find the most effective.

Да здравствует великое, непобедимое знамя
МАРКСА-ЭНГЕЛЬСА-ЛЕНИНА-СТАЛИНА!

Figure 8.2

It is important to note that some academics have questioned whether there is any genuine evidence for the effectiveness of these different learning styles. What is clear is that students should not simply identify themselves as one type of learner, and refuse to learn in a different style. Part of ensuring that students become successful lifelong learners is encouraging them to become flexible and able to learn in many different ways. They might be presented with information that does not fit their preferred style; for example, in the workplace a student who self-identifies as an auditory learner might be tasked with evaluating statistical data. Therefore, although reflection on preferences is important, students should be encouraged to try lots of different learning strategies so that they are adaptable.

Teacher Tip

Encourage your students to share their successful learning strategies with their peers. They could post advice on the school's Virtual Learning Environment, along with comments on how best to utilise it. Encourage teachers in other departments to do the same. This will create a constantly expanding bank of strategies that students can apply to a range of subjects.

LESSON IDEA 8.2: SHARING LEARNING STRATEGIES

Start a new topic by writing the enquiry question on the board.
Do not provide guidance on how best to answer it. Ask students
to individually plan and answer, then to share it with a pair, then a
group of four, then the whole class.

Write down all the ideas, on the board. Moderate the discussion
but avoid giving students the correct solution or correcting errors
in their thinking. Do not criticise solutions that are not effective,
but work through all the different solutions so that students can
see that learning is a process that requires reflection and planning,
and also a willingness to experiment with different strategies.

Ask students to explain why they approached the question in
the way they did. Communicate to them that in historical studies
there are different ways to come to an answer, and that a range of
interpretations can be equally valid.

**⊡ LESSON IDEA ONLINE 8.3: IDENTIFYING EFFECTIVE
LEARNING STRATEGIES**

This lesson idea is designed to allow students to consider a range
of approaches to a historical problem, and to consider which
learning strategies are more effective and why.

Encouraging students to reflect

Teachers play an important role in encouraging students to ask the kind
of questions that encourage them to reflect upon how they learn. Here
are some examples:

- What is this historical question asking me to do?
- What is the best way that I can ensure I remember this information?
- What did I do when I faced a similar question before? Did my
  approach work? ·
- What are the strengths of my usual learning approach? Why do I
  usually take this approach?
- What are the weaknesses? Why do I not like trying different approaches?
- What can I do if I get stuck?

Planning/monitoring/ evaluating

Planning

Students will need to be given time to plan which strategy they will apply to solve a given problem. A key aspect of metacognition is the ability to learn from previous lessons. Students should reflect upon times when they have been presented with a similar problem: how did they solve the problem? What worked well for them? Did they start off by using a strategy that was ineffective, and why? They should now consider what approach they will use for the problem on this occasion, and plan how they will implement their chosen strategy.

Monitoring

Students aware of their metacognition are thinking about how they are learning. During your class you could ask questions such as 'What are you doing, and why?' and 'Is what you are doing working? If not, how could you change it?' Encouraging them to monitor the effectiveness of their learning will help your students to build a range of strategies that they have reflected upon and can use when faced with the same kind of problem in the future.

Evaluating

The ability to engage effectively with teacher feedback and to make the adjustments necessary to improve is an important aspect of metacognition. Ask students to read over a previous assessment: do they understand why they got the mark that they did? Did they try the wrong approach? Were they disorganised – did they leave their revision to the last minute? Ask them to write down at least one thing that they will do differently next time.

🖳 LESSON IDEA ONLINE 8.4: WHAT FACTORS INFLUENCE YOU AS A HISTORIAN?

Examining the validity of historians' views and why they have changed is a common type of test for History students. This lesson

→

applies a metacognitive approach to the study of historians' interpretations; it encourages students to think about personal bias, to reflect upon what factors influence the way historians think, and also consider why students themselves think about History in the way they do.

Teacher Tip

Students may be nervous when they start to study a new topic. You can reassure them by starting the first lesson with a learning technique they have already used successfully and applying it to learning about the new topic. They will quickly see that although the factual content might be very different and unfamiliar, learning strategies which they have used previously can be successfully used again.

Summary

This chapter has focused on the importance of developing your students' metacognition. Look back over the material and reflect on the following:

- Are you providing students with time in lessons to reflect upon how best they learn?

- Do you encourage all students, regardless of ability, to engage in this kind of thinking?

- Do you take opportunities to encourage students to try out a number of learning strategies so that they are able to apply a range of strategies to different types of problems?

- Can you help students to understand the strengths and weaknesses of different strategies and to have the confidence to apply ones that they have not tried before?

Language awareness

9

What is language awareness?

For many students, English is an additional language. It might be their second or perhaps their third language. Depending on the school context, students might be learning all or just some of their subjects through English.

For all students, regardless of whether they are learning through their first language or an additional language, language is a vehicle for learning. It is through language that students access the learning intentions of the lesson and communicate their ideas. It is our responsibility as teachers to ensure that language doesn't present a barrier to learning.

One way to achieve this is to support our colleagues in becoming more language-aware. Language awareness is sensitivity to, and an understanding of, the language demands of our subject and the role these demands play in learning. A language-aware teacher plans strategies and scaffolds the appropriate support to help students overcome these language demands.

Why is it important for teachers of other subjects to be language-aware?

Many teachers are surprised when they receive a piece of written work that suggests a student who has no difficulties in everyday communication has had problems understanding the lesson. Issues arise when teachers assume that students who have attained a high degree of fluency and accuracy in everyday social English therefore have a corresponding level of academic language proficiency. Whether English is a student's first language or an additional language, students need time and the appropriate support to become proficient in academic language. This is the language that they are mostly exposed to in school and will be required to reproduce themselves. It will also scaffold their ability to access higher order thinking skills and improve levels of attainment.

What are the challenges of language awareness?

Many teachers of non-language subjects worry that there is no time to factor language support into their lessons, or that language is something they know little about. Some teachers may think that language support is not their role. However, we need to work with these teachers to create inclusive classrooms where all students can access the curriculum and where barriers to learning are reduced as much as possible. An increased awareness of the language needs of students aims to reduce any obstacles that learning through an additional language might present.

This doesn't mean that all teachers need to know the names of grammatical structures or need to be able to use the appropriate linguistic labels. What it does mean is that we all need to understand the challenges our students face, including their language level, and plan some strategies to help them overcome these challenges. These strategies do not need to take a lot of additional time and should eventually become integral to our process of planning, teaching and reflecting on our practice. We may need to support other teachers so that they are clear about the vocabulary and language that is specific to their subject, and how to teach, reinforce and develop it.

Language awareness for History students

Historical writing has its own unique vocabulary. Historians use it to define periods such as 'medieval' Europe or 'antebellum' America. Terms such as 'revolution' or 'dictatorship' have meant different things at different times in the past. A failure to identify and comprehend key terms in the study of the subject will lead to misunderstandings and jeopardise success in a student's course.

In this chapter we highlight some strategies you might use to support students for whom the language and terminology of History is new. Such strategies should help students whose first language is not English. We also consider the language demands of History exams, such as the key words used in typical essay questions and the specific language used to analyse, evaluate and compare historical sources.

How can you help build language skills?

There are many ways in which you can help students cope with the language demands of our subject. As you build language objectives into your lesson plans, consider using the following strategies to support your teaching.

Understanding students' learning backgrounds

You should be aware that students of diverse backgrounds or countries of origin may have very different definitions of key historical terminology. For example, terms such as 'democracy' or 'civil rights' may not mean the same thing to students of dissimilar backgrounds. Furthermore, the same events might have alternative names: Western nations refer to the 1939–1945 conflict as the Second World War, while students in Russia might refer to the war against Nazi Germany as

'The Great Patriotic War'. These nuances in language can be extremely significant and should be understood.

Being a role model

You will need to act as a role model in the use of correct historical terminology. When asking questions in class, you should mirror the language that students will encounter through their historical studies as well as that used in examination questions, so that students become accustomed to the correct terms. If you show them how to use and apply the correct terms, they will be more likely to use them when engaging with factual content. Make sure the correct terms are used in any handout that is given to students: you are trying to ensure that the use of historical terminology becomes second nature, so you must be careful to use the language correctly at all times.

Teacher Tip

Body language and tone of voice can help students to identify key terminology. Sometimes using gestures or lowering your voice to ensure students are compelled to listen carefully can help emphasise key terms.

Being precise in your use of historical terminology

Historical terms are not interchangeable. For example, an autocracy is not the same as a dictatorship, and an authoritarian ruler is not the same as a totalitarian one. You should not expect your students to automatically understand the nuanced differences, and you will need to be very clear in your use of these terms.

Identifying key historical vocabulary in advance

Provide a list of key terms to be used in the next lesson, setting students a homework task to familiarise themselves with them. Start the next lesson by checking students' understanding of the terms. This is particularly important at the beginning of the course when you are trying to develop students' historical vocabulary.

Teacher Tip

Providing an explanation of key terms in a glossary sheet can be a useful strategy to help students engage more actively in class and improve their performance. This can be especially important when dealing with the historical study of a different country or culture, when sometimes words in a foreign language are left untranslated.

Highlighting the essential language

Another technique to increase students' language awareness is to use a model or example answer to emphasise historical terms. Students could talk through an explanation or description of the historical issue and then write it up, underlining or using a different colour to pick out the historical terms.

The following is an example of a written extract, showing highlighted terms:

> Hitler started the **Second World War** because of his desire for **Lebensraum**. He believed that the Germanic **Aryan** race was superior to the **Untermensch**, the racial 'subhumans', such as the Jews. He felt that he was justified in seeking to overturn the **Versailles Treaty** as this had been a **stab in the back** that he damned as a 'dictated peace'.

Using this method, you will be helping your students to attain a good level of subject-specific language proficiency, rather than remaining in the conversational, non-technical language arena.

Assisting with era-specific language

Written language has changed greatly over time. Students may be asked to analyse, evaluate and compare sources written a long time ago, and the language may appear strange and archaic. For example, sources written in Tudor England or medieval Spain would use unfamiliar terminology, and church documents written during the Reformation would use religious phrases that have long since ceased to be commonly used. In such cases, providing key terms is especially important.

Allowing time to engage with historical interpretations

Grasping the differences between historical interpretations can be challenging, especially if English is not the student's first language. When setting reading tasks, make sure you give your class time not only to read a text, but also to engage with its unique interpretation and to decide on their own opinion of it.

Teacher Tip

Set tasks that focus on students pulling out the interpretations of a given text. Ask students to read a piece of historical writing carefully, highlighting the vocabulary the author uses to support their own argument and reject those of other historians. This kind of language can be useful when writing examination answers that typically ask students to compare historians' interpretations and to decide which one they find most convincing.

Giving students easier material to read

If students are finding a textbook challenging, you could suggest that they read a book that is more accessible – perhaps a book or website written to support students at an earlier stage in their education. The simplified text will help them develop a sound basic understanding before moving on to the more complex textbook.

Using classroom displays

Classroom displays can be used to help collate related words and prompt their use. For example, a display of East German propaganda posters can help students to understand how that Communist dictatorship endured for so long. Creating signs with key words to use as classroom displays can help remind students of the language they must use. Asking students to draw visual metaphors of key words or events on mini whiteboards can help you to measure their understanding.

Using puppet shows

If following complex text is challenging, turning that text into a visual medium can help students. Converting text into a simple puppet show can help students grasp confusing events. There are a range of computer apps that can help students create puppet shows.

LESSON IDEA 9.1: USING PUPPET SHOWS TO DEVELOP LANGUAGE COMPREHENSION

The arguments over whether Charles I, the King of England, should have been executed can be challenging to grasp. To help students, you could ask them to create a puppet show of the trial of the King. The physical representation of the trial can help understanding.

Checking understanding regularly

Make sure that the language is clear when working through any articles or handouts. Ask students to identify words that are unclear in any historical article you give them before the analysis and discussion begins. Even if English is their first language, you will often find terms in historical journals that are unfamiliar to them. Students can identify their own areas of uncertainty and compare what they know in pairs. Have regular tests that check understanding of key vocabulary.

Teacher Tip

When marking a piece of work that contains a lot of spelling or grammatical errors, focus on a small number of key errors. Consider using these as teaching points, explaining to the student how to avoid the error next time. When marking, try to explain the problem with an error and suggest solutions.

The language demands of the History exam

Historical writing requires students to interpret questions very precisely and produce arguments demonstrating skills that match the assessment objectives. In this section, we consider the importance of command words and the particular challenges of the higher-level skill questions that require analysis and evaluation.

Understanding command words

Command words are used in History examinations to make clear to the students how they should answer a question, so it is important that students understand fully what they mean.

Different command words require different skills. For example:

* A question that begins with 'Compare' requires students to give an account of the similarities or differences between events or historical figures.
* A 'How far do you agree?' question asks students to make a judgement as to how convincing they find an interpretation.

Teacher Tip

Check the syllabus and support materials for your course for a list of command words and what is required for each.

☑ LESSON IDEA ONLINE 9.2: HOW TO USE PAST PAPER QUESTIONS

Use this lesson to help students identify the key words in assessment questions, and to ensure that their answers engage with them.

Figure 9.1 shows some example command words and phrases used in History questions.

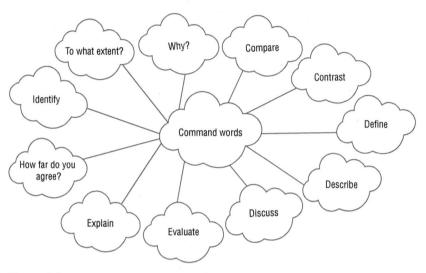

Figure 9.1

Understanding terms that describe historical concepts

History students need to understand how to address conceptual terms used by historians such as 'significance', 'continuity' or 'turning point'. For example, you will need to encourage students to reflect upon what makes an event 'significant'. This could include criteria such as the number of people affected by an event, or how long the impact lasts. A question such as 'How far was Henry VIII's closing of the monasteries a turning point for religion in England?' will require students to have a very clear understanding of how a 'turning point' can be identified.

Writing about historical sources

A typical history syllabus will ask students to analyse historical sources, whether primary sources from the period being studied, or secondary sources written by historians after the period.

There is a language particular to answering these questions. Students should avoid writing that a source 'says' or 'states' because this implies that a source is a fact, rather than an interpretation or opinion. Instead, they should refer to sources 'arguing', 'suggesting' or 'presenting a view'. They should write about the 'utility' or 'credibility' of a source and about how far an argument is 'persuasive' or 'convincing'. They should also avoid writing that a source is 'biased'. All sources are biased by definition: they are an interpretation written from one particular perspective. Instead, students should use terms such as 'political perspective' or 'vested interest'.

Useful words and phrases

Suggests; claims; argues; asserts; evaluates; theorises; debates; supports; corroborates; analyses; contradicts; slanted; one-sided; balanced; perspective; emphasises; interprets; implies; echoes; undermines; objective; subjective; believes.

- While X asserts that ... Y would argue that this is not the case.
- X claims that ... Y supports this in part when they argue that ...
- Both X and Y argue that ... This would suggest that more weight can be added to their claim ...
- X is correct in their claim that ...
- Y asserts that ... However, his claim is undermined by ...
- X asserts that ... Her claim can be supported by ...
- While Y acknowledges the validity of this argument, he prefers to emphasise ...

Teaching a new topic

If you are asked to teach a completely new topic in History, your first reaction may be to ensure that you have understood the subject content well yourself. You will probably start by making a checklist of the issues that are relevant to the topic, and the appropriate terminology. Equipped with this, you may feel ready to tackle the first lesson.

For example, if you are about to teach a unit on life in the German Democratic Republic, you might consider the following terms to be content-obligatory. As you can see, the need to be aware of language challenges is heightened because some content-specific terms will be in another language:

- Social contract
- Stasi
- Volkshammer
- Eingaben

Approaches to learning and teaching History

- Kirchenkampf
- Ostpolitik.

You might also need to think about the content–compatible language that you are about to use. Debates between historians have their own peculiar language. For example, historians have applied a range of terms to try to accurately describe how far the German people supported the Communist government. They use terms such as 'consent' and 'consensus' that sound similar but mean different things. There are terms such as 'niche society' whereby German citizens passively accepted Communist rule and focused on making the best of their private lives; or 'welfare dictatorship' where historians argue that the government tried to prevent opposition to their rule by providing social benefits. Before you start teaching topics where the terminology of the debate is important, you should understand fully the definition of key terms.

Summary

Look back on the material in this chapter and reflect on the following points:

- It is important that the language that you use in lessons is accessible to students of all backgrounds and abilities.

- Historians use a precise language; there are many strategies you can employ which will help students to understand this and to use it in their own work.

- Be a role model by using history-specific language throughout your lessons so that students become accustomed to it.

- Ensure your students understand the meaning of the command terms used in History questions, and the key historical terms that they will need to succeed in their course.

- Source analysis has its own vocabulary, which you will need to teach your students.

- Different historical topics have their own language characteristics – you will need to understand these before you begin to teach a topic.

Inclusive education

10

What is inclusive education?

Individual differences among students will always exist; our challenge as teachers is to see these not as problems to be fixed but as opportunities to enrich and make learning accessible for all. Inclusion is an effort to make sure all students receive whatever specially designed instruction and support they need to succeed as learners.

An inclusive teacher welcomes all students and finds ways to accept and accommodate each individual student. An inclusive teacher identifies existing barriers that limit access to learning, then finds solutions and strategies to remove or reduce those barriers. Some barriers to inclusion are visible; others are hidden or difficult to recognise.

Barriers to inclusion might be the lack of educational resources available for teachers or an inflexible curriculum that does not take into account the learning differences that exist among all learners, across all ages. We also need to encourage students to understand each others' barriers, or this itself may become a barrier to learning.

Students may experience challenges because of any one or a combination of the following:

* behavioural and social skill difficulties
* communication or language disabilities
* concentration difficulties
* conflict in the home or that caused by political situations or national emergency
* executive functions, such as difficulties in understanding, planning and organising
* hearing impairments, acquired congenitally or through illness or injury
* literacy and language difficulties
* numeracy difficulties
* physical or neurological impairments, which may or may not be visible
* visual impairments, ranging from mild to severe.

We should be careful, however, not to label a student and create further barriers in so doing, particularly if we ourselves are not qualified to make a diagnosis. Each student is unique but it is our management of their learning environment that will decide the extent of the barrier and the need for it to be a factor. We need to be aware of a student's readiness to learn and their readiness for school.

Why is inclusive education important?

Teachers need to find ways to welcome all students and organise their teaching so that each student gets a learning experience that makes engagement and success possible. We should create a good match between what we teach and how we teach it, and what the student needs and is capable of. We need not only to ensure access but also make sure each student receives the support and individual attention that result in meaningful learning.

What are the challenges of an inclusive classroom?

Some students may have unexpected barriers. Those who consistently do well in class may not perform in exams, or those who are strong at writing may be weaker when speaking. Those who are considered to be the brightest students may also have barriers to learning. Some students may be working extra hard to compensate for barriers they prefer to keep hidden; some students may suddenly reveal limitations in their ability to learn, using the techniques they have been taught. We need to be aware of all corners of our classroom, be open and put ourselves in our students' shoes.

Inclusion in the history classroom

As we study History, we learn about the human race; what it means to be a human being; our place in the scale of human history; what human beings are capable of. We also learn to put ourselves in perspective. As such, it is vital that no student is excluded or prevented from studying History on account of their particular learning needs.

Priorities and obligations

History at secondary level is often viewed as a challenging subject, requiring substantial reading and writing. However, it is important that our programmes of study are rooted in the needs of individual students in our classes, rather than just in assessment outcomes. As such, we need to ask ourselves important questions as to how we can meet their needs as learners:

- What allowances or adjustments can I undertake to make my classroom more inclusive?
- Can any changes be made to the topics taught in programmes of study to make them more accessible to students with specific learning needs?
- Can I work with other departments to help scaffold the skills which will support their learning in History? For example, could I liaise with the English department in coordinating the teaching of Civil Rights in the USA with the study of literary works, such as *To Kill a Mockingbird*?

Knowing your students' needs

A lack of understanding of the individual needs of students is often a primary cause of exclusion. Don't assume that all students, for instance, have the ability to make notes from a textbook or DVD, or even catch

up on work if they have been away from lessons through illness or a
school activity.

Teacher Tip

Assess your students' individual skill needs and address them,
while also taking into consideration any information about
hidden disabilities. Try to anticipate their needs and develop
your appreciation of what makes them more effective learners.
Running a survey with your class to enhance your understanding
of their own learning needs may be informative and productive.

Fundamentally, learning is a collaborative process. Try to share the
responsibility for supporting students with specific learning needs with
other colleagues. Talking to teachers in related subjects about approaches
to teaching and learning may help to develop new strategies which
will work for you. If your school has a learning support department,
seek their guidance and aid. You may have some baseline data regarding
your students' past performance. If so, use this as a source of evidence
to inform but not dictate your teaching. Remember that you have your
own data set in front of you in the form of both written work and,
importantly, engagement in class.

Building relationships between the school and students' parents or
guardians can also be a powerful strategy. There are lots of activities parents
can engage in at home to support the learning of their daughters and sons.

Teacher Tip

Make the most of support within the wider family to
reinforce students' learning. Their help in consolidating
learning from the classroom may prove invaluable. You might
encourage a family to watch a clip on the internet together,
and discuss the causes of a particular event or the significance
of an individual. A trip to a museum or other site of historical
interest may also be productive, especially if the student can
use the opportunity to develop a particular interest in an
issue or object, which may fire their enthusiasm for History
and boost self-esteem.

Classroom management

Approaching the management of a class in a way that assumes that all students have the same abilities and aptitudes is another common barrier to inclusion. We all learn in slightly different ways and a 'one style fits all' approach will fail to provide both the support and the extension opportunities your students need. Consider using a range of resources to meet their needs; for example, in exploring the origins of the Cold War, you might look at diagrams outlining international relations, but also draw on contemporary cartoons and movie clips.

Bear in mind that a textbook will rarely meet the needs of all students for all topics. Adapting resources or creating your own so that they are more carefully tailored to your students' needs will both benefit their learning and facilitate better classroom management. Concentration and engagement will improve if students are working with materials which best fit their needs. Worksheets with an uncluttered layout and a larger font, and with colour or highlighting for key pieces of information, often work best.

Teacher Tip

Remember that some students may have difficulty retaining information and instructions in their heads for long enough to act on them. For these students, it can be helpful to break down the information rather than giving instructions all at once. It can also be useful to repeat instructions and questions.

Although this strategy will support inclusion, actually all students benefit from clear instruction. Starting lessons with a clear outline of the tasks ahead is invariably a good plan. Consider writing the learning objectives clearly on the board. As the lesson progresses, you (and they!) can use this framework to test progress. This is an effective strategy to check an individual's understanding and offer praise accordingly. One version of this approach is to write tailored lesson objectives on a sticky note and place this on the desk of a student with particular needs. Remember that inclusion also means meeting the needs of the most confident students too, so this can be a useful strategy to achieve this goal.

Try to vary your grouping of students according to purpose and the nature of learning. Be careful to avoid seating arrangements which might lead to a group identifying themselves as being of 'low ability'. You will find that regular changes of your seating plan can help to avoid students being labelled or indeed labelling themselves as stronger or weaker learners. A thoughtful, sensitive classroom layout will be especially important to students with visual or audio difficulties. Think about where these students may best be able to participate fully in the lessons, and factor this in from the start of your course.

Differentiated teaching

Plan and prepare activities for groups, pairs and individuals rather than simply the whole class. Similarly, attempt to build differentiation into your preparation and have additional resources available. Remember that differentiation can come in many different forms. For example, you may wish to differentiate via setting different tasks, or providing students with a range of resources to tackle different types of question. Naturally, teachers also differentiate through the level of support needed to support students addressing challenging questions or topics. However, try to be flexible within your planning rather than being too prescriptive. This is especially important when preparing a series of lessons or a lengthier programme of study.

Teacher Tip

Think about strategies to consolidate learning. Supplying students with a one-sheet summary of the lesson and its learning outcomes may be productive. Similarly, some students would benefit from an audio file providing a brief overview. Whatever format you choose, help students organise or curate these materials.

Homework is an area that lends itself to a differentiated approach, and you may wish to consider setting different types of homework tasks. Some students may be more comfortable producing an audio answer rather than a more traditional written response. Others may prefer to produce their findings in a visual format through annotated diagrams.

The opportunity to submit work in different formats is likely to have a liberating impact on students. Displaying or publicly acknowledging the value and validity of different types of work allows for a more creative approach and promotes wider engagement.

Teacher Tip

Feel prepared to give your students greater flexibility regarding some homework tasks, offering them a range of options regarding how they present work.

For example, building on a study of the Peace Settlements following the First World War, you might ask the students to produce a revision resource on the impact of the respective treaties. This could vary from simple text revision notes to taking a visual form as a poster or flash cards; or it could even be an electronic resource such as a PowerPoint or an Explain Everything presentation. Make it clear to the students that the work will be assessed in terms of the accuracy, creativity and effort behind it.

Developing questioning skills

Reflect on how to promote debate and good questioning techniques. Some teachers have found 'flipping the classroom' to be a useful strategy. Here, rather than the teacher delivering content, students are expected to access this material as homework before coming to a lesson with the information necessary to debate a topic. 'Flipping the classroom' can help students generate their own questions about a topic and so may lead them to develop more complex lines of enquiry and generate some engaging homework tasks. Careful use of this strategy can build a useful hierarchy of questions.

Think about how you might scaffold students' enquiries by breaking down difficult questions to explore more complex issues. I had an exchange similar to the one below with a student studying Germany in the 1920s:

Student:	What exactly is democracy?
Teacher:	What do you understand it as being?
Student:	Not really sure. Something to do with the government, I suppose?

Teacher:	Well, the word democracy was originally a Greek term – *demokratia*. It means people power. So how much power did the people have in Weimar Republic?
Student:	People could vote in elections.
Teacher:	That's right. Well done. Which people could vote? Men? Women? What age?
Student:	I don't know. Men, yes. Women … maybe.
Teacher (to whole class):	Yes, almost there. Well done. Men and women over 20 could vote in elections. But what other sources of power were there?

The sequence of questions aims to scaffold the student towards an answer to the question and places their knowledge within a contemporary and historical context.

Think about how you might reinforce this outcome to the class.

Supporting language needs

Consider your strategies to support students whose difficulties stem from a different language or cultural background. Bear in mind that their problems may, in fact, be rather subtle. Naturally, students whose mother tongue is not English may encounter language difficulties without having a specific learning difficulty.

Do not assume that even relatively common vocabulary is precisely understood or fully appreciated within a given context. Complex sentence structures often take longer to retain and fully process – indeed, the students themselves may well not be fully aware that their actual understanding is partial. Consider checking a student's understanding of key concepts and vocabulary by asking them to explain a concept back to you in their own words. It also makes sense for you to reflect carefully on the use of idiomatic language in your teaching as well as in their writing.

Helping students move away from a colloquial or conversational style of historical writing may prove a particular challenge. Feel free to teach subject-specific vocabulary, and provide writing and thinking frameworks to help with this in particular. For more on language issues, look back to Chapter 9 **Language awareness**.

☑ **LESSON IDEA ONLINE 10.1: EXPLORING LANGUAGE FOR ASSESSING CAUSAL FACTORS**

This lesson aims to provide students with a background topic in which to explore scaffolding vocabulary for essay writing and debate.

☑ **LESSON IDEA ONLINE 10.2: USING LANGUAGE TO ASSESS CAUSATION, SIGNIFICANCE AND CHANGE/ CONTINUITY**

This lesson follows on from Lesson idea 10.1. It explores the use of other types of vocabulary to identify wider categories of historical language.

Using a question framework

Providing a question framework can be extremely helpful in enabling students to access the key aims of the lesson from the beginning. It creates a structure for the progression of skills and growth of confidence during the lesson itself. Such frameworks can also prove invaluable in helping all students to access and fully engage with homework tasks.

LESSON IDEA 10.3: QUESTION FRAMEWORKS

Give students a question such as 'Stalin's personal strengths were the main reason he became the leader of the Soviet Union. How far do you agree?'

- What exactly is meant by personal strengths?
- What other factors were there?
- What role did other individuals play in Stalin's rise?
- What other forces contributed to Stalin's rise?
- On balance, do you agree or disagree? What was the main factor in explaining Stalin's rise?

Students could respond to the question in different formats – as a traditional piece of historical writing, in a diagram or even as a movie clip or audio file.

Classroom displays and board use

History classrooms are often some the brightest and best resourced in a school, presenting students with lots of different stimuli, such as photographs, maps, artefacts and displays of work. This is all part of creating a dynamic environment which draws on sensory learning. While such a creative learning environment may meet the needs of many, it is important to recognise that this may not be the case for all. Some students, especially those with autism or who suffer from visual impairment, may find this distracting. Again the key is to know your students' needs. This may impact on your decision as to the seating plan for individual students.

Bear in mind the visibility of the whiteboard or screen in your classroom. Can all students see the full dimensions clearly, and are there any problems with glare at different times of the day? This may lead you to adjust the layout of the classroom to address these issues where possible. Consider, too, the impact of different colours. Students with dyslexia may find light lettering on a dark background extremely challenging to read; indeed, some research suggests that students with dyslexia find it easiest to read from cream backgrounds with dark blue writing, in a non-serif font. Some students may benefit from handouts with wider line spacing, too.

In addition, you might consider opportunities to present audio-visual materials in a more accessible manner. Remember that many video clips will have subtitled options, which can be useful. Similarly, remember the alt-text function where a word or phrase can be inserted as an attribute in an HTML (Hypertext Markup Language) document to tell website viewers the nature or contents of an image. Consider using this feature yourself in the production of electronic resources.

Trips and activities

However challenging the logistics may be, organising trips and activities outside the classroom brings benefits to all. Standing on a site of historical significance can have a deep intellectual, and indeed emotional, impact on students. It can create a shared experience from which creative, collaborative work may emerge. However, do remember that some students may find visiting some historical sites, for instance battlefields, profoundly emotionally disturbing, especially if they have a personal connection with the location.

These experiences can be particularly powerful for students who struggle to articulate their ideas in written form. Certainly, first-hand experiences outside the classroom can help to make learning deeper and build students' personal, social and emotional development alongside their historical understanding. For example, having taken students to the Somme for many years, I am struck by how many students feel their experience has helped them to empathise more deeply with their studies.

Ensuring the health and safety of all participants is naturally a critical obligation when organising and leading such activities. Preparatory visits are therefore important to assess the suitability of practical arrangements and contingency plans for all students, but especially those with more complex needs.

Summary

In this chapter we have looked at the ways in which inclusion can be achieved, and be of benefit to all students. Look back at the material to ensure your understanding of the following:

- Your students have a range of skills and aptitudes. They are all different, and it is important to acknowledge that different outcomes will stem from this.

- Careful scaffolding of questioning and written tasks alongside the setting of clear objectives will lead to better outcomes.

- Differentiation of tasks both in and outside the classroom and for homework will bring clear benefits.

Teaching with digital technologies

11

What are digital technologies?

Digital technologies enable our students to access a wealth of up-to-date digital resources, collaborate locally and globally, curate existing material and create new material. They include electronic devices and tools that manage and manipulate information and data.

Why use digital technologies in the classroom?

When used successfully, digital technologies have the potential to transform teaching and learning. The effective use of technology in the classroom encourages active learning, knowledge construction, inquiry and exploration among students. It should enhance an existing task or provide opportunities to do things that could not be done without it. It can also enhance the role of assessment, providing new ways for students to demonstrate evidence of learning.

New technologies are redefining relationships and enabling new opportunities. But there are also risks, so we should encourage our students to be knowledgeable about and responsible in their use of technology. Integrating technology into our teaching helps prepare students for a future rooted in an increasingly digitised world.

What are the challenges of using digital technologies?

The key to ensuring that technology is used effectively is to remember that it is simply a resource, and not an end in itself. As with the use of all resources, the key is not to start with the resource itself, but to start with what you want the student to learn. We need to think carefully about why and how to use technologies as well as evaluating their efficiency and effectiveness.

If students are asked to use digital technologies as part of their homework, it is important that all students are able to access the relevant technology outside school. A school needs to think about a response to any 'digital divide', because if technology is 'adding value', then all students need to be able to benefit. Some schools choose to make resources available to borrow or use in school, or even loan devices to students.

Safety for students and teachers is a key challenge for schools and it is important to consider issues such as the prevention of cyber-bullying, the hacking of personal information, access to illegal or banned materials and distractions from learning. As technology changes, schools and teachers need to adapt and implement policies and rules.

One of the greatest pitfalls is for a teacher to feel that they are not skilled technologists, and therefore not to try. Creative things can be done with simple technology, and a highly effective teacher who knows very little about technology can often achieve much more than a less effective teacher who is a technology expert. Knowing how to use technology is not the same as knowing how to teach with it.

Using digital technology effectively

The growth in access to digital resources has had a transformative impact on the practice of many History teachers. Certainly many (older) History teachers will recall the problems faced in the past in accessing information. The problem for our students today is one of information overload and selection. Consequently, we need to guide our students in developing effective strategies in assessing the utility and reliability of the information before them.

Figure 11.1: Sources of digital information.

Most teachers, whether experienced or relatively new to the profession, would probably recognise that we swiftly develop our own routines and, consequently, many of the things we do in the classroom can become second nature. Imaginative use of digital technology can thus be a powerful strategy to move out of our comfort zone. For example, many schools are equipped with interactive whiteboards, but I suspect that some highly experienced teachers fail to capitalise fully on their potential.

Our students live in an increasingly digital age. Teaching practice is evolving to make greater use of technology in the classroom, not only to promote the development of higher order skills, but also to foster a deeper understanding of the challenges and joys of the subject.

History teaching and digital literacy

Many students enjoy their study of History in the classroom, but often struggle to connect the skills they develop to real-world situations. For example, students develop their talents exploring inference, reliability and comparison of sources, but sometimes the application of these skills in a broader context seems limited. In the same way that we expect our students to examine sources critically, we must also help them critique information they find on the internet. Ask yourself:

• How can students be helped to use search engines effectively for historical material?
• How can they apply rigorous tests to the material they find online to assess its reliability and utility?
• How can they learn to be critically selective, identifying essential and non-essential information on the internet?

LESSON IDEA 11.1: PRESENTING EVIDENCE AND INTERPRETATIONS

The ability to be selective in the deployment of knowledge is an important skill. Ask students to produce a digital slideshow on a broad topic, representing the key ideas or features in a limited number of slides. What the students choose to leave out will need just as much reflection as what they include. Ask different groups within the class to discuss what they included and excluded, and why. This could then lead to a decision as to the information to be chosen for in the final, collective resource.

Teacher Tip

Many students often struggle to appreciate the connections between events or causal factors. Software such as Popplet can be a highly effective tool to help students explore the relationship between different themes and events. It is available for both PC and Apple platforms, and files can be exported as pdfs.

Making better use of digital resources

Many of us use productivity software such as spreadsheets or word-processing packages on a daily basis. Yet how can we make more imaginative use of these trusty resources to facilitate better learning, rather than simply to produce work? Here are some tips and lesson ideas which could work for you.

Beginnings and endings

All teachers seek to capture the full attention and engagement of students at the start and end of their lessons. Digital resources in many forms are a very good means to accomplish this. Some teachers might seek to achieve this visually, with a stimulating image on the board as students enter the room, or with a short video clip which sets out a framework of an event or debate.

One splendid resource which can add variety to lesson introductions is Socrative, an app available for PC, Apple or Android devices. Socrative is a dynamic quiz-based system, which is excellent for setting students initial questions on either a multiple-choice or yes/no basis. The teacher, via a separate app, is able to receive immediate feedback on students' performance and can tailor the development of the lesson accordingly.

Similarly, testing students' knowledge and understanding at the end of a lesson can be a very effective strategy to test outcomes. A concluding Socrative-based test can be a fun and useful mechanism to assess learning and act as a bridge into the following lesson.

Teacher Tip

If all of your class have smartphones, you might wish to consider using these rather than laptops or tablets. You could even prepare a series of Socrative quizzes as useful and engaging revision resources.

Using presentation software effectively

Many History teachers make very effective use of software such as
Slides or PowerPoint. However, often a presentation which looks fine
on a desktop will not always be attractive on a screen or a whiteboard.
Ensuring each slide has a legible font and is not too cluttered will help
your students focus on the key information. This will also be important
in building an inclusive classroom environment. Similarly, thinking
about the colours you use for text while also checking the resolution of
images will help to avoid 'death by PowerPoint'!

Encouraging learning through visual methods

Finding the most suitable images to promote learning is a great way to
engage your students. The internet has opened up access to a wide array
of visual materials for use in the classroom.

LESSON IDEA 11.2 UNLOCKING VISUAL MEMORY

Ask your class to put together a series of photos to unlock their
visual memories. Task groups of students to collate images on
topics and use these to produce posters or presentations. With
good annotations, these can be excellent revision resources for the
class to share.

An innovative approach is to make use of movie-making software, such
as Movie Maker for PC or iMovie for Apple devices, where students
can work collaboratively to represent their findings digitally. This can
be particularly rewarding for those who struggle with complex writing
tasks but excel at presenting their work in a visual format.

Constructing a digital storyboard may be an effective strategy in
encouraging students to reflect on historical processes and connections.
Here, digital media, in the form of stills or video, can be used to present
information regarding an event or to explain an idea or concept. This
can provide an excellent vehicle for historical research, and promotes
teamwork and debate. One approach might be to give students a case
study to investigate – for example, the Cuban Missile Crisis of 1962 –
and ask them to explore its consequences.

Another possible approach is to use Apple Clips to provide short animated revision videos with the opportunity to integrate images, music and text. Clips can then be uploaded to a range of platforms including YouTube, iMessage and Instagram. (While YouTube can be a useful resource, make sure to supervise your students to ensure that they do not access any inappropriate content.) Some students may find this a useful revision focus for the study of key individuals in particular.

Using spreadsheets

Think about how you might use spreadsheet software in lessons too. For example, you could ask students to use spreadsheets to examine statistics, as in Lesson idea 11.3.

> **🖳 LESSON IDEA ONLINE 11.3: USING DATA**
> This lesson idea suggests using spreadsheet software to analyse data and present the results.

Engaging learners actively in their use of such data will help them to remember key statistics and to appreciate their importance.

Harnessing geographical resources

Using Google Earth may prove a stimulating way of developing students' appreciation of how geographical considerations have impacted on historical developments. For example:

- You could use place marks in Google Earth to chart the implementation of the Schlieffen Plan at the start of the First World War, and explore how the plan failed.
- A study of the Vietnam War would be greatly enhanced by developing students' understanding of the terrain of South East Asia, giving them a deeper appreciation of different campaigns.
- Students often struggle to grasp the scale of large countries such as China or Russia. Using place marks to chart the problems facing Tsardom during the 1905 Revolution would be a useful tool in addressing this, providing a geographical overview of challenges which could then be assessed in chronological order.

Digital resources and collaborative learning

Google Drive and Google Classroom are both fantastic resources to encourage collaborative work. Students can use Google Drive to share work with their teachers, who can then annotate this in real time. This is a tremendously useful means of providing feedback. Audio files can also be a very useful strategy to help students refine their work.

Teacher Tip

You might consider giving small groups of students an essay to annotate digitally. Individuals could examine and annotate a paragraph individually, before turning to look at the whole essay as a group. A further strategy might be to give students answers to questions and then ask them to colour-code evidence, analysis and judgements in answers. They could share their findings on a platform such as Google Drive.

Approaches such as these may prove especially useful in promoting both individual engagement and collaborative working.

Digital resources and building an inclusive classroom

Confidence in the use of a wide range of digital resources varies among teachers. However, it is important to appreciate that the same applies to our students. While some will be extremely talented in their use of a wide range of platforms, others will be far more hesitant. To bridge this gap, you might consider appointing a small number of students in each class as 'digital champions'. Placing a more confident student in groups where there is more limited familiarity with resources, or pairing some of the most able with less proficient students, will help to build a more inclusive and skilled classroom.

Teacher Tip

Apple has a whole series of programmes to help teachers develop confidence with digital resources. You may also find it helpful to explore the opportunities provided by Google Educator Groups, communities of educators aim to learn, share and inspire each other to meet the needs of their students through technology solutions, both in the classroom and beyond.

Extending and supporting students with digital resources

At times, it can be challenging to meet the needs of the whole class, aiding students who are struggling with a topic yet also stretching other, more confident students. Digital technologies provide opportunities to support both groups. There are now many resources available to challenge able and committed young historians.

The BBC Radio 4 series *In Our Time* has an excellent online archive of history-related discussion where leading academics explore the impact of individuals and key historical events from around the world. These programmes range from 30 to 50 minutes, and can be streamed online or downloaded as podcasts. Consider playing one or two to a History Club, or encouraging students to listen to different programmes and then write a review for others in the class.

Many students will benefit from resources which reinforce their learning. There are lots of short summary video clips on the internet which focus on 'essential' learning points. These materials can be used effectively to consolidate learning and reinforce the understanding of all students.

You may also find it useful to encourage your school of college to subscribe to collections of online resources. A number of History journals suitable for students in the 11–18 age range are available through subscriptions, which give you access to an online archive of past articles.

Digital resources can be especially useful in meeting the challenge of preparing students to study History at a higher level. Cambridge University has an excellent set of resources available for keen historians to develop their powers of source evaluation of both primary sources and the work of modern scholars. This 'Virtual Classroom' also includes a series of online lectures. Students can work through these resources at their own pace, and there is plenty of guidance to help build their skills of historical analysis. This is a terrific resource for students wishing to study at a world-leading institution, but the materials could also be adapted for those with different ambitions.

History teaching and social media

Twitter or another social media platform can be an excellent resource, both inside and out of the classroom. One colleague, who ran a History bookclub, encouraged his students to tweet their thoughts on their text as they read each chapter. It proved a very effective tool to motivate students, and encouraged them to venture their own ideas in a clear, concise and very personal manner.

Twitter also offers outstanding opportunities for teachers who are looking for new ideas to implement in the classroom. Being part of a wider digital community can be especially helpful if you are a member of a small History or Humanities department.

LESSON IDEA 11.4 BUILDING BIOGRAPHICAL KNOWLEDGE

The majority of our students now have a number of social media profiles, and quite a few of their teachers have the same. Think about using the concept of a social media profile to developing your students' biographical knowledge of key individuals for a period you are studying in depth. For example, if you are studying Russia in the 1920s and 1930s, students could write Instagram-style profiles for the most prominent political figures, with a series of images to illustrate their careers. These could then be used as a presentation to the class or as display materials.

Creating a history blog for your class can be an effective way to promote student engagement, and allow you and your students to exchange information and share ideas with the wider community. One former colleague of mine established a local history blog which she used to encourage students to visit local historical sites and post their own reflections and images. A good strategy would be to choose your target audience carefully, which should help you to encourage committed students to become active participants. Of course, you could use it as part of a wider research task too.

Digital resources and 'the flipped classroom'

'Flipped learning' or 'the flipped classroom' has been an area of great debate in many schools in recent years. It encourages knowledge gathering as a homework activity, with activities and discussions being the focus in the classroom – the exact opposite of what we usually do. One very helpful resource which might help you explore this is Explain Everything, an app which allows teachers and students to access material simultaneously. The teacher can produce a resource with a range of slides along with embedded video and audio. This can be an excellent way to introduce a topic as a homework task, which can enable more targeted use of time in the classroom.

Plagiarism and digital resources

Finally, any discussion of digital resources must include an important point about plagiarism. An enormous range of history resources on the internet provides access for our students to huge quantities of material. This is a great aid to the student but it can also bring dangers. Some may be tempted to cut and paste information from the internet and present this as their own work; in certain cases, this might stem from a lack of understanding as to what constitutes plagiarism as well as deliberate malpractice. Coursework assignments probably prove the greatest temptation of all and it is here that the greatest penalties can lie. Not only may the student be failed for their whole examined History course, but potentially for a whole series of examinations. As such, you should explain clearly what is and what is not acceptable practice and, in particular, check word-processed work carefully.

- Does it reflect the student's normal manner of working?
- Are they able to explain the arguments presented and provide evidence of access to the sources they present?

If you have concerns, you will need to consult your examination officer and follow the guidance of the relevant examination board. To help ensure that the work students submit is free from plagiarism, consider using software to identify this, such as turnitin.

Teacher Tip

Do remember to ensure that you are familiar with your school's ICT policy and follow the guidance offered. This should ensure that both you and your students follow good practice.

Summary

This chapter has focused on the impact of digital technology on the teaching of History. Look back over the material presented and reflect on the following questions:

- Many teachers are equipped with the digital tools, but are you reflecting on the craftsmanship required to make the most of these?

- Do you stress the importance of developing digital skills with your students rather than placing the emphasis on knowing all there is to know about specific historical topics?

- Do you feel confident and enthusiastic about using digital technology in the classroom and encouraging your students to do the same?

12 | Global thinking

What is global thinking?

Global thinking is about learning how to live in a complex world as an active and engaged citizen. It is about considering the bigger picture and appreciating the nature and depth of our shared humanity.

When we encourage global thinking in students we help them recognise, examine and express their own and others' perspectives. We need to scaffold students' thinking to enable them to engage on cognitive, social and emotional levels, and construct their understanding of the world to be able to participate fully in its future.

We as teachers can help students develop routines and habits of mind to enable them to move beyond the familiar, discern that which is of local and global significance, make comparisons, take a cultural perspective and challenge stereotypes. We can encourage them to learn about contexts and traditions, and provide opportunities for them to reflect on their own and others' viewpoints.

Why adopt a global thinking approach?

Global thinking is particularly relevant in an interconnected, digitised world where ideas, opinions and trends are rapidly and relentlessly circulated. Students learn to pause and evaluate. They study why a topic is important on a personal, local and global scale, and they will be motivated to understand the world and their significance in it. Students gain a deeper understanding of why different viewpoints and ideas are held across the world.

Global thinking is something we can nurture both within and across disciplines. We can invite students to learn how to use different lenses from each discipline to see and interpret the world. They also learn how best to apply and communicate key concepts within and across disciplines. We can help our students select the appropriate media and technology to communicate and create their own personal synthesis of the information they have gathered.

Global thinking enables students to become more rounded individuals who perceive themselves as actors in a global context and who value diversity. It encourages them to become more aware, curious and interested in learning about the world and how it works. It helps students to challenge assumptions and stereotypes, to be better informed and more respectful. Global thinking takes the focus beyond exams and grades, or even checklists of skills and attributes. It develops students who are more ready to compete in the global marketplace and more able to participate effectively in an interconnected world.

What are the challenges of incorporating global thinking?

The pressures of an already full curriculum, the need to meet national and local standards, and the demands of exam preparation may make it seem challenging to find time to incorporate global thinking into lessons and programmes of study. A whole-school approach may be required for global thinking to be incorporated in subject plans for teaching and learning.

We need to give all students the opportunity to find their voice and participate actively and confidently, regardless of their background and world experiences, when exploring issues of global significance. We need to design suitable activities that are clear, ongoing and varying. Students need to be able to connect with materials, and extend and challenge their thinking. We also need to devise and use new forms of assessment that incorporate flexible and cooperative thinking.

Global thinking and History

There is often heated debate as to the importance of teaching the history of one's nation as opposed to that of others. Where should the balance lie in the teaching of History between 'the national story' as opposed to wider continental or even global histories?

It is frequently claimed that the study of History helps us to understand the present. Having an appreciation of global history may therefore be viewed as a necessity in helping us address the challenges of today and tomorrow. In our globalised culture, it is natural that we should look beyond national or regional boundaries to explore wider issues. As the eminent Cambridge historian Christopher Bayley put it, 'All historians are world historians now, though many have not yet realized it'.

What is global history?

Some of the broader themes you can explore with your classes include:

- history of a nation or regions within a global context
- imperialism and its impact
- movement of peoples
- contact and dialogue.

Teacher Tip

It is easy to ignore anything that is not in the syllabus you are studying and focus on the materials that the student needs to know. Of course, it is right that the main focus is on the topic of study, but contextual or comparative information can help students engage with the subject matter, and may help them remember the materials specified.

Our place in the world

Many teachers will find that their best resources in exploring global issues in History are their own students, who originate from or have lived in different parts of the world. Accounts of their own personal histories and appreciation of the history of their own countries can be an excellent starting point in encouraging global thinking.

LESSON IDEA 12.1: DEVELOPING A GLOBAL OUTLOOK

Use the experiences of your students to examine the historical topics they have studied in different parts of the world. You could map the countries your students have studied and discuss why some parts of the world are the focus of greater historical study than others. To what extent, for example, do History courses look at Asian and African history through a study of imperialism?

Controversial matters

Studying global history may lead you to examine some deeply controversial and sensitive topics, an issue touched upon in Chapter 10 **Inclusive education**. Many school History courses will include case studies in genocide, for example. Issues such as these can be difficult to study in a detached academic sense, and you may well feel that this would be inappropriate anyway. As historians, our challenge is, through rigorous scrutiny, to uncover as closely as possible what actually happened, while being conscious and sensitive to the human impact of events.

Teacher Tip

Most students studying the Nazis or the Second World War will explore acts of genocide. Consider placing these events within a broader chronological and geographical spectrum by examining other case studies – for example, in Cambodia and Rwanda. You could analyse the accounts of survivors to identify similarities and differences in experience, and how these events have been commemorated.

The Holocaust Memorial Day Trust has some excellent resources for educators and students.

Connected classroom

Establishing relations with other schools around the world can be an excellent platform for students and teachers to exchange ideas about the study of History. Students can compare different courses and approaches to historical study, and consider deeper questions relating to the nature of the subject.

LESSON IDEA 12.2: A GLOBAL APPROACH TO THE FIRST WORLD WAR

A great deal of History teaching relating to the First World War focuses on events from a Eurocentric perspective, and overlooks or gives very limited treatment to experiences of men and women outside Europe or North America. Ask your students how many nations contributed troops who fought in the war. Many students will be surprised by the answer and the numbers of combatants from Asia, Africa and Australasia who fought and died in the conflict.

Figure 12.1: Indian cavalry at the battle of the Somme, 1916.

LESSON IDEA 12.3: IMPACT OF GLOBAL ECONOMIC DEPRESSION

A common area of study for students is the impact of the Wall Street Crash and the resulting global economic depression. However, students' exploration of this issue is often rooted in the impact of the Depression on the USA, Britain, Germany and Japan. Consider some micro studies of the impact on other countries too. Research homework examining the impact of global depression on India, Australia and South American countries, especially Chile, would be instructive. You could follow this up with a mapping exercise charting the impact of the Depression across the globe and assessing the relative degree of impact.

🖳 LESSON IDEA ONLINE 12.4: FAMINES IN HISTORY

This lesson idea can be adapted to many topics. It is a good way of getting students to examine specific incidences within a wider historical context.

Global history projects

The study of global history particularly lends itself to project work, with groups of students researching the impact and significance of developments. This can be a valuable tool to challenge preconceptions about the speed of change in differing parts of the world. For example, you might consider the development and impact of ideas and approaches to medical care or the evolving nature of warfare. One colleague of mine led a fascinating project with her class, examining the evolution of print.

The history of medicine

Many students particularly enjoy the study of the history of medicine. One especially fascinating area to examine is the impact of the outbreak of Spanish influenza at the end of the First World War. Students may also find it interesting to compare the reaction to Spanish influenza with the response to the outbreak of the H5N1 virus in Hong Kong in 1997 or current outbreaks of the Ebola virus.

Teacher Tip

An investigation of this nature can also be instructive in emphasising the interdisciplinary nature of the history of medicine. The study of Spanish influenza requires students to draw on an understanding of History, Geography, demography and medical data. It also provides a good opportunity for students to understand the complex issues facing historians in assessing the scale of casualties. For example, debate still rages as to the numbers of people who actually died from influenza as opposed to other conditions, such as diphtheria.

The history of sport

Global events such as the Olympic Games, football World Cup or Athletics World Championships are a splendid backdrop to explore the use of sport for propaganda purposes. Many students will be able to relate to this issue on a contemporary basis, making it easier to place these ideas within a wider historical context. Students may enjoy exploring the origins of sports such as rugby or cricket in a study of imperialism.

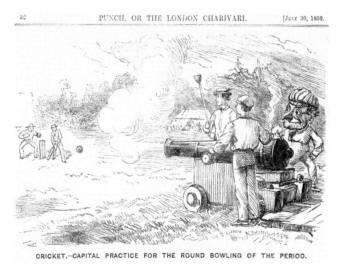

Figure 12.2: A satirical cartoon showing a cannon used in a game of cricket, commenting on Britain's foreign policy in the mid 19th Century.

An examination of competing nations and medal tables from the Olympic Games between 1948 and 1998 can prove the basis for students to raise questions about global change. This can be a useful way to generate broad questions which can then be explored thematically.

⧉ LESSON IDEA ONLINE 12.5: SPORT AND HISTORY

In this lesson, students can use the study of sport to explore the cultural influences some countries have had over others, as well as to explore themes of collaboration in History.

Calendar systems

Many students may assume that there is only 'one' calendar system and have a limited awareness of alternative models. Introducing students to these by examining Muslim and Hindu calendars, for example, will help to encourage a broader outlook. A useful tool of comparison is to look at the key events of the Crusader era and the different chronologies used.

Teacher Tip

Prepare a series of timelines exploring technological developments in Europe, the Middle East, China and India over the past three thousand years. This can be a very useful classroom resource for students to compare the nature and pace of change, and challenge some preconceptions.

Global thinking and biographies

Many History courses focus on the actions of individuals, with students developing a detailed knowledge of figures such as Mao, Stalin, Castro and Mandela. Encourage your students to research a wider range of individuals, some of whom are often overlooked in most History courses at this level. Students studying the Vietnam War could be encouraged to examine the military skills of Vo Nguyen Giap or the life of Kim Phuc, the so-called Napalm girl whose suffering was captured in a famous photograph of 1972. In short, try to seize opportunities to explore some lesser-known stories at this level. You could use this as a chance to explore the topics and individuals which feature prominently in History courses and why this is so.

Mapping the world

For most students to think globally in historical terms, they need to be able to visualise the world. A range of maps, both physically in the classroom and as electronic resources, are essential tools for History teachers. While many will be used to demonstrate changing political boundaries, also look for maps which chart population movement or the spread of diseases such as the Black Death. A varied display of maps in the classroom will be a good approach, but do not overlook the tremendous opportunities offered by electronic resources too. For example, you could create historical tours using Google Earth.

Remember that maps can be excellent revision resources for your students. Google Earth provides opportunities to create interactive and fun revision resources.

Summary

This chapter has focused on the importance of global thinking in the teaching of History. Look back over the material you have read and reflect on the following:

- Are you making the most of your global knowledge and understanding in your teaching in the classroom?

- Do you take opportunities to encourage students to think in global rather than just in national or continental terms and produce work which reflects this?

- By encouraging students to take a global perspective, can you help them understand their place in an interconnected world?

13 Reflective practice

Dr Paul Beedle, Head of Professional Development Qualifications, Cambridge International

'As a teacher you are always learning'

It is easy to say this, isn't it? Is it true? Are you bound to learn just by being a teacher?

You can learn every day from the experience of working with your students, collaborating with your colleagues and playing your part in the life of your school. You can learn also by being receptive to new ideas and approaches, and by applying and evaluating these in practice in your own context.

To be more precise, let us say that as a teacher:

* you **should** always be learning
  to develop your expertise throughout your career for your own fulfilment as a member of the teaching profession and to be as effective as possible in the classroom.
* you **can** always be learning
  if you approach the teaching experience with an open mind, ready to learn and knowing how to reflect on what you are doing in order to improve.

You want your professional development activities to be as relevant as possible to what you do and who you are, and to help change the quality of your teaching and your students' learning – for the better, in terms of outcomes, and for good, in terms of lasting effect. You want to feel that 'it all makes sense' and that you are actively following a path that works for you personally, professionally and career-wise.

So professional learning is about making the most of opportunities and your working environment, bearing in mind who you are, what you are like and how you want to improve. But simply experiencing – thinking about and responding to situations, and absorbing ideas and information – is not necessarily learning. It is through reflection that you can make the most of your experience to deepen and extend your professional skills and understanding.

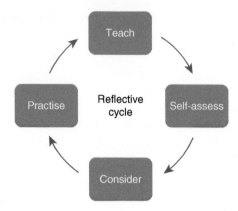

Figure 13.1

In this chapter, we will focus on three *essentials* of reflective practice, explaining in principle and in practice how you can support your own continuing professional development:

1 **Focusing** on what you want to learn about and why.
2 **Challenging** yourself and others to go beyond description and assumptions to critical analysis and evaluation.
3 **Sharing** what you are learning with colleagues – to enrich understanding and enhance the quality of practice.

These essentials will help you as you apply and adapt the rich ideas and approaches in this book in your own particular context. They will also help you if you are, or are about to be, taking part in a Cambridge Professional Development Qualification (Cambridge PDQ) programme, to make the most of your programme, develop your portfolio and gain the qualification.

1 Focus
In principle

Given the multiple dimensions and demands of being a teacher, you might be tempted to try to cover 'everything' in your professional development but you will then not have the time to go beneath the surface much at all. Likewise, attending many different training events will certainly keep you very busy but it is unlikely that these will simply add up to improving your thinking and practice in sustainable and systematic ways.

Teachers who are beginning an organised programme of professional learning find that it is most helpful to select particular ideas, approaches and topics which are relevant to their own situation and their school's priorities. They can then be clear about their professional learning goals, and how their own learning contributes to improving their students' learning outcomes. They deliberately choose activities that help make sense of their practice with their students in their school and have a clear overall purpose.

It is one thing achieving focus, and another maintaining this over time. When the going gets tough, because it is difficult either to understand or become familiar with new ideas and practices, or to balance learning time with the demands of work and life, it really helps to have a mission – to know why you want to learn something as well as what that something is. Make sure that this is a purpose which you feel genuinely belongs to you and in which you have a keen interest, rather than it being something given to you or imposed on you. Articulate your focus not just by writing it down but by 'pitching' it to a colleague whose opinion you trust and taking note of their feedback.

In practice

- Plan
  What is my goal and how will I approach the activity?

  Select an approach that is new to you, but make sure that you understand the thinking behind this and that it is relevant to your students' learning. Do it for real effect, not for show.

- Monitor
  Am I making progress towards my goal; do I need to try a different approach?

  Take time during your professional development programme to review how far and well you are developing your understanding of theory and practice. What can you do to get more out of the experience, for example by discussing issues with your mentor, researching particular points, and asking your colleagues for their advice?

- Evaluate
  What went well, what could have been better, what have I learned for next time?

  Evaluation can sometimes be seen as a 'duty to perform' – like clearing up after the event – rather than the pivotal moment in learning that it really is. Evaluate not because you are told you have to; evaluate to make sense of the learning experience you have been through and what it means to you, and to plan ahead to see what you can do in the future.

This cycle of planning, monitoring and evaluation is just as relevant to you as a professional learner as to your students as learners. Be actively in charge of your learning and take appropriate actions. Make your professional development work for you. Of course your professional development programme leaders, trainers and mentors will guide and support you in your learning, but you are at the heart of your own learning experience, not on the receiving end of something that is cast in stone. Those who assist and advise you on your professional development want you and your colleagues to get the best out of the experience, and need your feedback along the way so that if necessary they can adapt and improve what they are devising.

2 Challenge

In principle

Reflection is a constructive process that helps the individual teacher to improve their thinking and practice. It involves regularly asking questions of yourself about your developing ideas and experience, and keeping track of your developing thinking, for example in a reflective journal. Reflection is continuous, rather than a one-off experience. Being honest with yourself means thinking hard, prompting yourself to go beyond your first thoughts about a new experience and to avoid taking for granted your opinions about something to which you are accustomed. Be a critical friend to yourself.

In the Cambridge PDQ Certificate in Teaching and Learning, for example, teachers take a fresh look at the concepts and processes of learning and challenge their own assumptions. They engage with theory and models of effective teaching and learning, and open their minds through observing experienced practitioners, applying new ideas in practice and listening to formative feedback from mentors and colleagues. To evidence in their assessed portfolio how they have learned from this experience, they not only present records of observed practice but also critical analysis showing understanding of how and why practices work and how they can be put into different contexts successfully.

The Cambridge PDQ syllabuses set out key questions to focus professional learning and the portfolio templates prompts to help you. These questions provide a framework for reflection. They are open-ended and will not only stimulate your thinking but lead to lively group discussion. The discipline of asking yourself and others questions such as 'Why?' 'How do we know?' 'What is the evidence?' 'What are the conditions?' leads to thoughtful and intelligent practice.

In practice

Challenge:

- Yourself, as you reflect on an experience, to be more critical in your thinking. For example, rather than simply describing what happened, analyse why it happened and its significance, and what might have happened if conditions had been different.
- Theory – by understanding and analysing the argument, and evaluating the evidence that supports the theory. Don't simply accept a theory as a given fact – be sure that you feel that the ideas make sense and that there is positive value in applying them in practice.
- Convention – the concept of 'best practice(s)' is as good as we know now, on the basis of the body of evidence, for example on the effect size of impact of a particular approach on learning outcomes (defined in the next chapter). By using an approach in an informed way and with a critical eye, you can evaluate the approach relating to your particular situation.

3 Share

In principle

Schools are such busy places, and yet teachers can feel they are working on their own for long periods because of the intensity of their workload as they focus on all that is involved in teaching their students. We know that a crucial part of our students' active learning is the opportunity to collaborate with their peers in order to investigate, create and communicate. Just so with professional learning: teachers learn best through engagement with their peers, in their own school and beyond. Discussion and interaction with colleagues, focused on learning and student outcomes, and carried out in a culture of openness, trust and respect, helps each member of the community of practice in the school clarify and sharpen their understanding and enhance their practice.

This is why the best professional learning programmes incorporate collaborative learning, and pivotal moments are designed into the programme for this to happen frequently over time: formally in guided learning sessions such as workshops and more informally in opportunities such as study group, teach meets and discussion, both face-to-face and online.

In practice

Go beyond expectations!

In the Cambridge PDQ syllabus, each candidate needs to carry out an observation of an experienced practitioner and to be observed formatively themselves by their mentor on a small number of occasions. This is the formal requirement in terms of evidence of practice within the portfolio for the qualification. The expectation is that these are not the only times that teachers will observe and be observed for professional learning purposes (rather than performance appraisal).

However, the more that teachers can observe each other's teaching, the better; sharing of practice leads to advancement of shared knowledge and understanding of aspects of teaching and learning, and development of agreed shared 'best practice'.

So:

- open your classroom door to observation
- share with your closest colleague(s) when you are trying out a fresh approach, such as an idea in this book
- ask them to look for particular aspects in the lesson, especially how students are engaging with the approach – pose an observation question
- reflect with them after the lesson on what you and they have learned from the experience – pose an evaluation question
- go and observe them as they do the same
- after a number of lessons, discuss with your colleagues how you can build on your peer observation with common purpose (for example, lesson study).
- share with your other colleagues in the school what you are gaining from this collaboration and encourage them to do the same
- always have question(s) to focus observations and focus these question(s) on student outcomes.

Pathways

The short-term effects of professional development are very much centred on teachers' students. For example, the professional learning in a Cambridge PDQ programme should lead directly and quickly to changes in the ways your students learn. All teachers have this at heart – the desire to help their students learn better.

The long-term effects of professional development are more teacher-centric. During their career over, say, 30 years, a teacher may teach many thousand lessons. There are many good reasons for a teacher to keep up-to-date with pedagogy, not least to sustain their enjoyment of what they do.

Each teacher will follow their own career pathway, taking into account many factors. We do work within systems, at school and wider level, involving salary and appointment levels, and professional development can be linked to these as requirement or expectation. However, to a significant extent teachers shape their own career pathway, making decisions along the way. Their pathway is not pre-ordained; there is room for personal choice, opportunity and serendipity. It is for each teacher to judge for themselves how much they wish to venture. A teacher's professional development pathway should reflect and support this.

It is a big decision to embark on an extended programme of professional development, involving a significant commitment of hours of learning and preparation over several months. You need to be as clear as you can be about the immediate and long-term value of such a commitment. Will your programme lead to academic credit as part of a stepped pathway towards Masters level, for example?

Throughout your career, you need to be mindful of the opportunities you have for professional development. Gauge the value of options available at each particular stage in your professional life, both in terms of relevance to your current situation – your students, subject and phase focus, and school – and the future situation(s) of which you are thinking.

14 Understanding the impact of classroom practice on student progress

Lee Davis, Deputy Director for Education,
Cambridge International

Introduction

Throughout this book, you have been encouraged to adopt a more active approach to teaching and learning and to ensure that formative assessment is embedded into your classroom practice. In addition, you have been asked to develop your students as meta-learners, such that they are able to, as the academic Chris Watkins puts it, 'narrate their own learning' and become more reflective and strategic in how they plan, carry out and then review any given learning activity.

A key question remains, however. How will you know that the new strategies and approaches you intend to adopt have made a significant difference to your students' progress and learning? What, in other words, has been the impact and how will you know?

This chapter looks at how you might go about determining this at the classroom level. It deliberately avoids reference to whole-school student tracking systems, because these are not readily available to all schools and all teachers. Instead, it considers what you can do as an individual teacher to make the learning of your students visible – both to you and anyone else who is interested in how they are doing. It does so by introducing the concept of 'effect sizes' and shows how these can be used by teachers to determine not just whether an intervention works or not but, more importantly, *how well* it works. 'Effect size' is a useful way of quantifying or measuring the size of any difference between two groups or data sets. The aim is to place emphasis on the most important aspect of an intervention or change in teaching approach – the **size of the effect** on student outcomes.

Consider the following scenario:

Over the course of a term, a teacher has worked hard with her students on understanding 'what success looks like' for any given task or activity. She has stressed the importance of everyone being clear about the criteria for success, before students embark upon the chosen task and plan their way through it. She has even got to the point where students have been co-authors of the assessment rubrics used, so that they have been fully engaged in the intended outcomes throughout and can articulate what is required before they have even started. The teacher is happy with developments so far, but has it made a difference to student progress? Has learning increased beyond what we would normally expect for an average student over a term anyway?

Here is an extract from the teacher's markbook.

Student	Sept Task	Nov Task
Katya	13	15
Maria	15	20
Joao	17	23
David	20	18
Mushtaq	23	25
Caio	25	38
Cristina	28	42
Tom	30	35
Hema	32	37
Jennifer	35	40

Figure 14.1

Before we start analysing this data, we must note the following:

- The task given in September was at the start of the term – the task in November was towards the end of the term.
- Both tasks assessed similar skills, knowledge and understanding in the student.
- The maximum mark for each was 50.
- The only variable that has changed over the course of the term is the approaches to teaching and learning by the teacher. All other things are equal.

With that in mind, looking at Figure 14.1, what conclusions might you draw as an external observer?

You might be saying something along the lines of: 'Mushtaq and Katya have made some progress, but not very much. Caio and Cristina appear to have done particularly well. David, on the other hand, appears to be going backwards!'

What can you say about the class as a whole?

Calculating effect sizes

What if we were to apply the concept of 'effect sizes' to the class results in Figure 13.1, so that we could make some more definitive statements about the impact of the interventions over the given time period? Remember, we are doing so in order to understand the size of the effect on student outcomes or progress.

Let's start by understanding how it is calculated.

An effect size is found by calculating 'the standardised mean difference between two data sets or groups'. In essence, this means we are looking for the difference between two averages, while taking into the account the spread of values (in this case, marks) around those averages at the same time.

As a formula, and from Figure 14.1, it looks like the following:

$$\text{Effect size} = \frac{\text{average class mark (after intervention)} - \text{average class mark (before intervention)}}{\text{spread (standard deviation of the class)}}$$

In words: the average mark achieved by the class *before* the teacher introduced her intervention strategies is taken away from the average mark achieved by the class *after* the intervention strategies. This is then divided by the standard deviation[1] of the class as a whole.

---

[1] The standard deviation is merely a way of expressing by how much the members of a group (in this case, student marks in the class) differ from the average value (or mark) for the group.

Inserting our data into a spreadsheet helps us calculate the effect size as follows:

	A	B	C
1	Student	September Task	November Task
2	Katya	13	15
3	Maria	15	20
4	Joao	17	23
5	David	20	18
6	Mushtaq	23	25
7	Caio	25	38
8	Cristina	28	42
9	Tom	30	35
10	Hema	32	37
11	Jennifer	35	40
12			
13	Average mark	23.8 = AVERAGE (B2:B11)	29.3 = AVERAGE (C2:C11)
14	Standard deviation	7.5 = STDEV (B2:B11)	10.11 = STDEV (C2:C11)

Figure 14.2

Therefore, the effect size for this class $= \dfrac{29.3 - 23.8}{8.8} = 0.62$
But what does this mean?

Interpreting effect sizes for classroom practice

In pure statistical terms, a 0.62 effect size means that the average student mark **after** the intervention by the teacher, is 0.62 standard deviations above the average student mark **before** the intervention.

We can state this in another way: the post-intervention average mark now exceeds 61% of the student marks previously.

Going further, we can also say that the average student mark, post-intervention, would have placed a student in the top four in the class previously. You can see this visually in Figure 14.2 where 29.3 (the class average after the teacher's interventions) would have been between Cristina's and Tom's marks in the September task.

This is good, isn't it? As a teacher, would you be happy with this progress by the class over the term?

To help understand effect sizes further, and therefore how well or otherwise the teacher has done above, let us look at how they are used in large-scale studies as well as research into educational effectiveness more broadly. We will then turn our attention to what really matters – talking about student learning.

Effect sizes in research

We know from results analyses of the Program for International Student Assessment (PISA) and the Trends in International Mathematics and Science Study (TIMMS) that, across the world, a year's schooling leads to an effect size of 0.4. John Hattie and his team at The University of Melbourne reached similar conclusions when looking at over 900 meta-analyses of classroom and whole-school interventions to improve student learning – 240 million students later, the result was an effect size of 0.4 on average for all these strategies.

What this means, then, is that any teacher achieving an effect size of greater than 0.4 is doing better than expected (than the average) over the course of a year. From our earlier example, not only are the students making better than expected progress, they are also doing so in just one term.

Here is something else to consider. In England, the distribution of GCSE grades in Maths and English have standard deviations of between 1.5 and 1.8 grades (A★, A, B, C, etc.), so an improvement of one GCSE grade represents an effect size of between 0.5 and 0.7. This means that, in the context of secondary schools, introducing a change in classroom practice of 0.62 (as the teacher achieved above) would result in an improvement of about one GCSE grade for each student in the subject.

Furthermore, for a school in which 50% of students were previously attaining five or more A★–C grades, this percentage (assuming the effect size of 0.62 applied equally across all subjects and all other things being equal) would rise to 73%.

Now, that's something worth knowing.

What next for your classroom practice? Talking about student learning

Given what we now know about 'effect sizes', what might be the practical next steps for you as a teacher?

Firstly, try calculating 'effect sizes' for yourself, using marks and scores for your students that are comparable, e.g. student performance on key skills in Maths, Reading, Writing, Science practicals, etc. Become familiar with how they are calculated so that you can then start interrogating them 'intelligently'.

Do the results indicate progress was made? If so, how much is attributable to the interventions you have introduced?

Try calculating 'effect sizes' for each individual student, in addition to your class, to make their progress visible too. To help illustrate this, let us return to the comments we were making about the progress of some students in Figure 14.1. We thought Cristina and Caio did very well and we had grave concerns about David. Individual effect sizes for the class of students would help us shed light on this further:

Student	September Task	November task	Individual Effect Size
Katya	13	15	0.22*
Maria	15	20	0.55
Joao	17	23	0.66
David	20	18	-0.22
Mushtaq	23	25	0.22
Caio	25	38	1.43
Cristina	28	42	1.54
Tom	30	35	0.55
Hema	32	37	0.55
Jennifer	35	40	0.55

* The individual 'effect size' for each student above is calculated by taking their September mark away from their November mark and then dividing by the standard deviation for the class – in this case, 8.8.

Figure 14.3

If these were your students, what questions would you now ask of yourself, of your students and even of your colleagues, to help you understand why the results are as they are and how learning is best achieved? Remember, an effect size of 0.4 is our benchmark, so who is doing better than that? Who is not making the progress we would expect?

David's situation immediately stands out, doesn't it? A negative effect size implies learning has regressed. So, what has happened, and how will we draw alongside him to find out what the issues are and how best to address them?

Why did Caio and Cristina do so well, considering they were just above average previously? Effect sizes of 1.43 and 1.54 respectively are significantly above the benchmark, so what has changed from their perspective? Perhaps they responded particularly positively to developing assessment rubrics together. Perhaps learning had sometimes been a mystery to them before, but with success criteria now made clear, this obstacle to learning had been removed.

We don't know the answers to these questions, but they would be great to ask, wouldn't they? So go ahead and ask them. Engage in dialogue with your students, and see how their own ability to discuss their learning has changed and developed. This will be as powerful a way as any of discovering whether your new approaches to teaching and learning have had an impact and it ultimately puts data, such as 'effect sizes', into context.

Concluding remarks

'Effect sizes' are a very effective means of helping you understand the impact of your classroom practice upon student progress. If you change your teaching strategies in some way, calculating 'effect sizes', for both the class and each individual student, helps you determine not just *if* learning has improved, but by *how much*.

They are, though, only part of the process. As teachers, we must look at the data carefully and intelligently in order to understand 'why'. Why did some students do better than others? Why did some not make any progress at all? Use 'effect sizes' as a starting point, not the end in itself.

Ensure that you don't do this in isolation – collaborate with others and share this approach with them. What are your colleagues finding in their classes, in their subjects? Are the same students making the same progress across the curriculum? If there are differences, what might account for them?

In answering such questions, we will be in a much better position to determine next steps in the learning process for students. After all, isn't that our primary purpose as teachers?

Acknowledgements, further reading and resources

This chapter has drawn extensively on the influential work of the academics John Hattie and Robert Coe. You are encouraged to look at the following resources to develop your understanding further:

Hattie, J. (2012) *Visible Learning for Teachers – Maximising Impact on Learning*. London and New York: Routledge.

Coe, R. (2002) *It's the Effect Size, Stupid. What effect size is and why it is important*. Paper presented at the Annual Conference of The British Educational Research Association, University of Exeter, England, 12–14 September, 2002. A version of the paper is available online on the University of Leeds website.

The Centre for Evaluation and Monitoring, University of Durham, has produced a very useful 'effect size' calculator (available from their website). Note that it also calculates a confidence interval for any 'effect size' generated. Confidence intervals are useful in helping you understand the margin for error of an 'effect size' you are reporting for your class. These are particularly important when the sample size is small, which will inevitably be the case for most classroom teachers.

15 Recommended reading

For a deeper understanding of the Cambridge approach, refer to the Cambridge International website (http://www. cambridgeinternational.org/teaching-and-learning) where you will find the following resources:

Implementing the curriculum with Cambridge: a guide for school leaders.

Developing your school with Cambridge: a guide for school leaders.

Education Briefs for a number of topics, such as active learning and bilingual education. Each brief includes information about the challenges and benefits of different approaches to teaching, practical tips, lists of resources.

Getting started with ... These are interactive resources to help explore and develop areas of teaching and learning. They include practical examples, reflective questions, and experiences from teachers and researchers.

For further support around becoming a Cambridge school, visit cambridge-community.org.uk.

The resources in this section can be used as a supplement to your learning, to build upon your awareness of History teaching and the pedagogical themes in this series.

Arthur, J. and Philips, R. (eds) (2000) *Issues in History Teaching.* London: Routledge.

Bentley-Davies, C. (2010) *How to be an Amazing Teacher.* Bancyfelin: Crownhouse Publishing.

Clarke, S. (2005) *Formative Assessment in the Secondary Classroom.* London: Hodder Education.

Davies, P., Lynch, D. and Davies, R. (2003) *Enlivening Secondary History: 40 Classroom Activities for Teachers and Pupils.* London: RoutledgeFalmer.

Eastwood, L., Coates, J. and Dixon, L. (et al.) (2009) *A Toolkit for Creative Teaching in Post-compulsory Education.* Maidenhead: Open University Press.

Evans, R.J. (2002) *Telling Lies about Hitler: The Holocaust, History and the David Irving Trial.* London: Verso Books.

Fisher, P., Wilkinson, I. and Leat, D. (2002) *Thinking Through History.* Cambridge: Chris Kington Publishing.

Grey, P., Little, R., Macpherson, R. and Etty, J. (2017) *Cambridge IGCSE History Option B: The 20th Century Coursebook*. Cambridge: Cambridge University Press.

Husbands, C., Kitson, A. and Pendry, A. (2003) *Understanding History Teaching: Teaching and Learning about the Past in Secondary Schools*. Maidenhead: Oxford University Press.

Lightbody, B. (2009) *Outstanding Teaching and Learning 14–19*. Batley: Collegenet ltd.

Lipstadt, D. (2016) *Denying the Holocaust: The Growing Assault On Truth and Memory*. London: Penguin.

Macmillan, M. (2009) *The Uses and Abuses of History*. London: Profile Books.

Muijs, D. and Reynolds, D. (2005) *Effective Teaching: Evidence and Practice*. London: Sage Publications.

Murphy, J. (2005) *100 Ideas for History Teaching*. London: Continuum.

Oakes, S. and Griffin, M. (2016) *The A-Level Mindset: 40 Activities for Transforming Student Commitment, Motivation and Productivity*. Bancyfelin: Crownhouse Publishing.

Perkins, D. (2009) *Making Learning Whole: How Seven Principles of Teaching can Transform Education*. San Francisco: Jossey-Bass.

Philpott, J. (2009) *Captivating your Class: Effective Teaching Skills*. London: Continuum.

Tarr, R. (2016) *A History Teaching Toolbook: Practical Classroom Strategies*. CreateSpace Independent Publishing Platform, 2016.

Thomas, E. (2017) *Outstanding History Lessons*. London: Bloomsbury.

Walker, L. (2008) *The Essential Guide to Lesson Planning*. Harlow: Pearson.

Watkins, C. (2015) *Meta-Learning in Classrooms*. The SAGE Handbook of Learning. Edited by Scott D. and Hargreaves E. London: Sage Publications.

Wragg, E.C. and Brown, G. (2001) *Questioning in the Secondary School*. London: Routledge.

Index

Approaches to learning and teaching History

inclusive education (*cont*)
  definition of, 84–85
  developing questioning
    skills, 90–91
  differentiated teaching,
    89–90
  importance of, 85
  knowing your students'
    needs, 86–87
  supporting language needs,
    90–91
individuals
  effect sizes, 133
  roles of, 20

journalism, 11
justifications, 11

knowledge, 6
  exploration of, 15

language, 7
  needs, 91–92
  skills, 74
language awareness, 7, 72
  challenges of, 73
  command words, 79–80
  era-specific language, 76–77
  historical concepts, 80
  historical interpretations, 77
  for history students, 74
  identifying historical
    vocabulary, 75–76
  skills, 74
  students' learning
    backgrounds, 74–75
  use of historical
    terminology, 75
  words and phrases, 81
  writing about historical
    sources, 80–81
learning, 2
  active, 41
  aims of, 26
  approaches to, 6
  barriers to, 6
  in classroom, 28–29
  collaborative, 103
  preferences, 66–68
  process of, 5, 6
  strategies, 68
  styles, 67
  through visual methods,
    101–102

Marwick, Arthur, 11
metacognition, 6
  awareness of, 65
  definition of, 62–63
  encouraging students to
    reflect, 68
  evaluating, 69
  learning preferences, 66–68
  monitoring, 69
  phases involved in, 62–63
  planning, 69
  skills, 63–64
metacognitive learners, 62

nature of subject, teaches
  history, 9–10

openness, 9
oral feedback, 56

peer assessment, 57–58
peer teaching, 41
phrases, 81
plagiarism, 106–107
planning, 69
primary sources, 32
professional development
  activities, 119
professional learning, 3, 119
professional skills, 119

question framework, 92–93
questioning
  in classroom, 51–52
  skills, 90–91
questions of significance,
  19–20

reflection, questions for, 49–50
reflective practice, 119–120
  challenge, 122–123
  essentials of, 120
  focus, 120–122
  pathways, 124–125
  share, 123–124

schools, 123
  key challenge for, 97
scope of discipline, 13
skills, 6, 63–64
  vs. knowledge, 28
  language, 74
  questioning, 90–91
social media, 105–106

student learning, 131, 132–134
  talking about, 132–134
students, 132–134
  to develop, 65
  engagement, 59
  extending and supporting,
    104–105
  learning, 2, 74–75
  progress and learning, 127
  size of effect, 127
  success criteria, 54
supplementary materials, 29
supplementary resources, 30
syllabus, 2, 31
  assessment objectives, 26
  definition of, 25–27
  planning your teaching,
    30–32
  selecting resources, 28–29
  supporting information, 27
  teaching support, 26

teacher
  role of, 43–44, 58–59
teaching, 2
  approaches to, 6
  aspects of, 3
  differentiated, 89–90
  methodology, 2
  planning, 30–32
  processes of, 5, 30
technology, advantages and
  challenges, 7
thinking
  about causation, 17–18
  about change and
    continuity, 19
  about significance, 19–20
tolerance, 9
Twitter, 105

visual methods, 101–102

Watkins, Chris, 128

Zeldin, Theodore, 9

140